PLANTS *of the* VIRGIN MOUNTAINS

A Guide to Common Wildflowers, Cacti, Trees and Shrubs of Arizona's Virgin Mountains

Frank J. Smith
Illustrations by Lee H. Rentz

Joshua Tree

To newcomers, the desert often appears austere and forbidding. But like any other landscape, it has its admirers; people who love its moods, its thunderstorms, and the feel of open sky all around. To these "desert rats", the plants are especially interesting, with their unusual adaptations and unexpectedly colorful flowers.

The purpose of this guide is to introduce both travelers and nearby residents to the plants of the Virgin Mountains. The sketches and descriptions include the most common and colorful plants visitors are likely to see.

Whatever the reason you came to this part of the Southwest, be sure to take some time to explore the canyons and mountain slopes. Look for the wildflowers. Investigate the natural communities. The experiences you have will remain with you as vivid memories of the living desert.

A PATHFINDER BOOK REPRINT EDITION

Originally prepared by the Bureau of Land Management. In this updated edition, January 2016, scientific names have been updated to those now generally accepted.

Printed in the United States of America

ISBN: 978-1951682446

Contents

INTRODUCTION

    First Impressions 1

    Plant Patterns in the Virgin Mountains 2

    Identifying Plants 6

    Picture Glossary 8

    The Meanings of Flowers 11

    Photographing Wildflowers 13

DESCRIPTIONS 15

    Trees and Shrubs 16

    Cacti and Cactus-like Plants 44

    Herbaceous Plants 56

REFERENCES 82

INDEX 83

REMOVING PLANTS 85

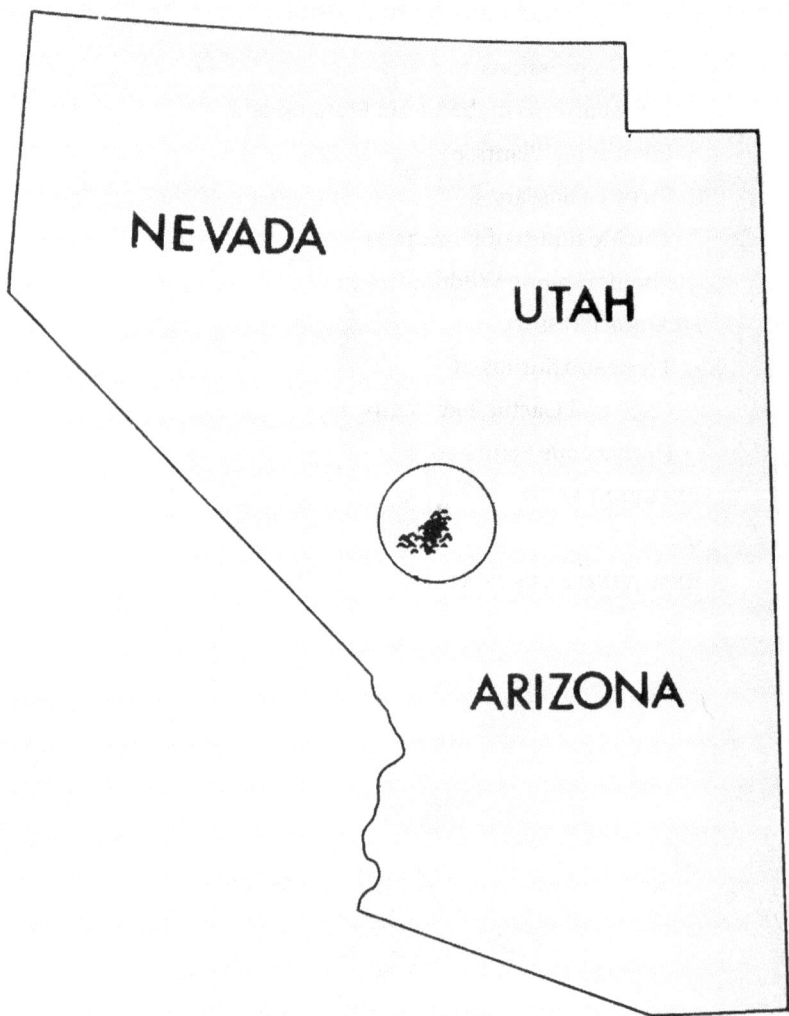

Location of the Virgin Mountains

First Impressions of the Virgin Mountains

When people drive through the Virgin River Gorge heading for Las Vegas, Los Angeles, or Salt Lake City, they briefly encounter an absurdly barren land. Plants, if noticed at all, seem subordinate to the massive rock walls. Lifeless rock threatens to squeeze out the life-giving light of the sun.

But these first impressions of the Virgin Mountains are deceiving. There is actually a very rich and interesting variety of plant life, ranging from the Joshua tree and cactus communities of the low desert to the pine and fir forests of the high mountains. Enhancing this natural variety is the loneliness of the landscape; the Virgins have seldom been visited by anyone other than ranchers, hunters, and early Indians. Botanists and naturalists face exciting challenges in exploring the secluded peaks and canyons. A recent botanical survey, for instance, revealed several unusual kinds of plants; one of which has probably never been seen by botanists before. The area is so rugged and wild that a portion of it was designated the Paiute Primitive Area.

The remote location of the Virgin Mountains has much to do with their past "neglect." Located in the extreme northwestern corner of Arizona (as shown on the Location Map), this mountain range was a barrier to travel in the past. Travelers had to take a detour up into Utah and through a pass at the north end of the Beaver Dam Mountains. I-15 changed that when the section through the Virgin River Gorge opened in 1973. Now travelers and hikers have easy access to the Virgin Mountains and the Paiute Primitive Area.

The Virgin Mountains stand between two great geological regions. The Basin and Range Region is found to the west and the Colorado Plateau Region to the east. This geological mix seems to provide a greater variety of habitats for plants than would be found in either geological region alone.

Additionally, the Virgin Mountains are found at the center of a variety of ecological regions. The Mohave Desert is immediately to the west, while the cold sagebrush deserts are found to the north and east. The mountains are high enough to provide refuge for an island of ponderosa pine forests and pinyon-juniper forests. The highest peak, Mt. Bangs at 8012 feet, is even partially clothed with north country forests of Douglas fir and white fir.

Plant Patterns in the Virgin Mountains

In midsummer, desert dwellers like to load up with cool drinks, swim trunks and fishin' poles and head for the mountains. You can't blame them; when temperatures are pushing 110 degrees in the shade and the hum of air conditioners becomes unbearable, the shady pine forests surrounding clear mountain lakes seem awfully tempting.

Plants, unlike people and some other animals, can't migrate to a milder environment when temperatures reach an extreme. And of course, they don't need to. Their ancestors lived in similar environments and gradually adapted to the extremes of heat and cold, drought and flood they encountered. Each species developed built-in ways of surviving the predictable stresses of its environment.

These built-in characteristics "trap" a plant species in a certain kind of environment. Mountain plants would be poorly adapted to survive in dry, hot deserts; conversely, desert plants could not stand the prolonged mountain winters.

Since the Virgin Mountains rise over 6,000 feet above the Mohave Desert, you would expect climatic differences between the base and the summit. Indeed, the differences in precipitation and temperature are very

Plant Communities Change With Elevation

As elevation increases, the environmental conditions of moisture and temperature also change. As a result, the natural communities are different at different elevations.

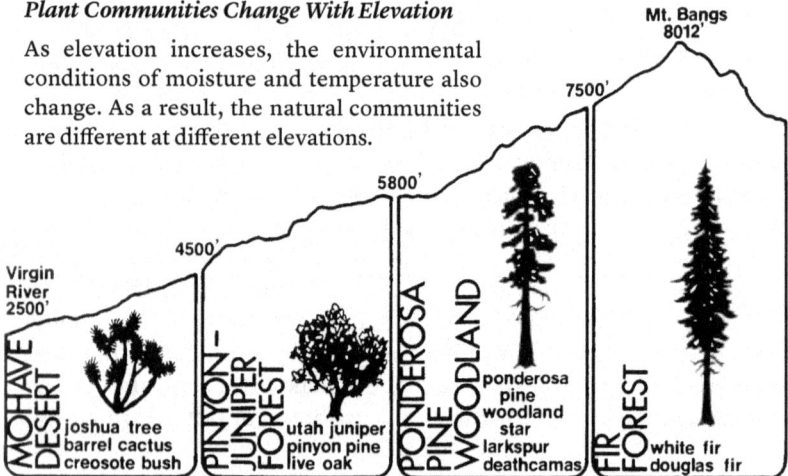

Mt. Bangs
8012'

7500'

5800'

4500'

Virgin
River
2500'

MOHAVE DESERT
joshua tree
barrel cactus
creosote bush

PINYON-JUNIPER FOREST
utah juniper
pinyon pine
live oak

PONDEROSA PINE WOODLAND
ponderosa
pine
woodland
star
larkspur
deathcamas

FIR FOREST
white fir
douglas fir

large. Near the settlement of Beaver Dam, just northwest of the Virgins, rainfall averages about 6 inches per year. In contrast, Mt. Bangs, the highest peak in the Virgin Mountains, averages nearly 20 inches of precipitation each year. The average, 24-hour July temperature at Beaver Dam is 88 degrees, while the average atop Mt. Bangs is 65 degrees — 23 degrees cooler! It is said that every 1,000 foot increase in elevation is accompanied by a 3 degree dip in the average yearly temperature. No wonder desert people migrate to the mountains on summer weekends.

As every traveler knows, the natural communities change as you drive up a road leading into the mountains. The cacti and creosote bushes give way to pinyon pines and junipers, which in turn give way to cool conifer forests. In other parts of the West, this progression of communities continues up into the alpine meadows of the real high country. But in the Virgin Mountains, ponderosa pine and Douglas fir forests clothe the highest slopes.

If you cut an imaginary slice through the Virgin Mountains, as in Figure 1, you will find that on each side, there are distinct zones of vegetation corresponding to the rise in elevation.

Ecologists find three major zones in the Virgins: (1) the Mohave Desert; (2) the Pygmy Forest of pinyon pine and junipers; and (3) the Ponderosa Pine Woodland. Each has a characteristic "look" derived from the plants found there.

The Mohave Desert occupies the canyons and long gravelly slopes surrounding the Virgin Mountains. The most unique plants are the Joshua trees; but the common inhabitants include barrel cacti, creosote bushes, prickly pear cacti and chollas. Of necessity, the plants are widely-spaced with shallow, spreading roots that soak up the brief rains. The plants are adapted in other ways to the pervading dryness. Cacti, for example, have thick, water-storing stems; waxy stem surfaces; dense, sunlight - reflecting white spines; sunken pores that close during the heat of the day; and mucilaginous sap that grabs and holds water absorbed by the plant. Other plants have different strategies for survival. Many annual wildflowers lie dormant in the soil as seeds for many years. When the right combination of time and rain wash a chemical inhibitor from the seed coat, the seed sprouts. Usually, this results in a scattered, sparse wildflower crop. But occasionally, the rains are gentle enough and long enough to produce bumper crops of poppies, evening primroses, sand verbenas and a myriad of other wildflowers. This only happens once or twice per decade, but when it happens, the drab desert earth is set on fire with brilliant, saturated colors. City people drive miles and miles to see the blooming desert on these rare occasions.

The low desert rarely experiences snow; most of its moisture comes as widely-scattered, small showers. Some of these showers are so explosive in nature that the rain merely slides off the soil surface into the gullies, resulting in flash floods. Plants are able to get little or none of this water. They prefer the steady, gentle, all-night rains that come in early spring.

The Pygmy Forest, in contrast, depends more upon winter snows. The slowly melting snows gradually give up their moisture to the soil. There it lies protected under a deep mulch of dried pine and juniper needles.

The Pygmy Forest is still a dry environment, but it gets enough moisture to support a very different complement of plants than the hot desert. The basic form of the forest is created by singleleaf pinyon pine and Utah juniper trees. They are short trees, hence the name "Pygmy Forest" is appropriate. Shrubs and herbs grow in the openings between the widely-spaced trees; but little grows in the dense shade under the trees.

The Pygmy Forest, more than any other environment in this region, supported large numbers of Indians. Food was probably the biggest reason for this. Winters brought deer to these forests; and fall brought the crop of pinyon pine nuts that so many people depended on.

The Pygmy Forest occupies a belt from 4,500 to about 5,700 feet in the Virgins. Above this belt, there is a transition to the forests of the high country. In some places, this transition zone is occupied by clumps of Gambel oak surrounded by mountain brush. In other places, manzanita and other shrubs densely cover the mountainsides. These brushy communities are probably only temporary; they came in after a forest fire destroyed a large tract of ponderosa pine. But the extensive brushlands will probably occupy these lands for years to come.

The most typical natural community along the Virgin Ridge and atop Black Rock Mountain is the ponderosa pine woodland. Like urban parks, these woodlands are composed of tall, widely spaced trees separated by broad, open spaces. A few delicate wildflowers grace the pine needle carpeted spaces between the trees.

Winter's snow cover leaves the cold pine forest relatively late because the trees' branches block out the warm rays of the sun. On north-facing mountain slopes, the sun penetrates to the ground only a few hours each day, so the snow takes even longer to melt. These slopes support scraggly stands of Douglas fir and white fir.

Until now, our picture of the Virgin Mountains vegetation has been a broad one. It could have been observed by looking at the land through an airplane window.

But up close, the natural communities are more like a mosaic of different, but related, parts. Look at the area around the Virgin River

Canyon campground, for instance. This area is all called Mohave Desert; but the pattern of vegetation isn't homogenized. Along the river there are masses of water-loving plants like tamarisk, desert willow and Arizona ash. On the sharp, rocky slopes between the river and the campground, barrel cacti and purple torch cacti are common. On the flat plain near the river, creosote bush dominates the community; while on the rocky hillsides above the campground, Joshua trees raise their tortured limbs. The Mohave Desert seems anything but uniform.

What causes these differences? We saw how changes in moisture and temperature change the flora. But these changes were on a big scale. Many changes in moisture, temperature, soil type and sunlight change the flora on a more local basis. These kinds of local changes are responsible for the mosaic of communities right around the campground.

The rich variety of plants surrounding springs is a good example of how a bountiful water supply affects plants. From a distance you can recognize springs by their leafy green look — even when they're surrounded by a stark, dry desert. Up close, you get an immediate impression of damp earth; of mosses and ferns and liverworts that are absent elsewhere. There are thickets of trees and shrubs: cottonwoods, sumacs, ashes and willows. The lasting impression is one of an oasis; which it indeed is.

A final aspect of plant ecology, the impacts of man on the Virgin Mountains, is particularly interesting. Since these mountains have been used mostly for grazing, cattle have probably had the biggest man-caused influence. You can see plants that have been nibbled, but most of the effects, such as changes in the kinds of plants, are subtle. The campground itself will provide an interesting study of grazing for visitors. Since the campground was fenced off to prohibit access by cows, its vegetation won't be grazed — but the vegetation outside the fence will. Compare the difference.

Another easily observed change is caused by roads. When it rains, water drains off the road onto a narrow strip on each side. During the year, this strip receives more moisture than the adjacent desert soils; so the plants grow larger. Some plants, like globemallow and tumbleweed, grow along this roadside strip — but not at all on the nearby desert.

Other vegetational changes near the campground are due to bulldozer scars, "people paths," tent sites and artificial plantings of native plants. Many of the changes are subtle, but can be observed by perceptive visitors.

Identifying Plants

To identify any plant, ask yourself a series of questions about its characteristics; then compare what you see with what the booklet says. It doesn't work to try to identify most plants on the basis of one characteristic, such as a leaf or the shape of the flower. Instead, you have to compare each of the most important characteristics listed in the description and shown in the drawing. Does the leaf have the same shape? Is it the right time of year to be flowering? Is the flower's shape the same? Is the fruit (if present) correct? Confirm every detail possible before deciding for sure what the plant is.

For your convenience, this booklet is divided into three categories. When you want to identify a plant, the first step is to place it in one of these categories:

(1) **Trees and Shrubs**
    All plants with woody stems fall into this category.

(2) **Cacti and Cactus-Like Plants**
    These plants, including true cacti, yuccas and agave are characterized by thick, water-storing stems or leaves.

(3) **Herbaceous Plants**
    These are annual or perennial plants that die back beneath the ground surface each year.

Within each of these categories, the plants are ordered by flower color (except for pines and other trees that have inconspicuous flowers). White-flowered plants are listed first; followed by cream, yellow, orange, red, pink, purple, blue and green. Once you've determined the flower color; you've narrowed the possibilities to, at most, 5 or 6 choices. Then it is a matter of comparing drawings and descriptions with the plant you want to identify.

If the tree, shrub or cactus you've found lacks flowers, the process becomes a little more difficult. Then you have to go through the appropriate section page by page, comparing the leaves, fruits, or other characteristics with the plant descriptions.

The descriptions themselves contain three types of information. First, they indicate where a particular plant grows in terms of soil and elevation. For example, a description might read: "A plant of sandy washes at elevations from 2,000 to 4,500 feet." This tells you where to expect the

plant. If you find an otherwise similar plant growing on a rocky mountain top at an elevation above 8,000 feet, it is probably a different species.

Secondly, each plant is described. Is it a shrub — or a perennial herb? How tall is it? Are the leaves opposite or alternate? How big is the flower? How many stamens and petals does it have? . . . and so on. The purpose is not to completely describe a plant; only to give the characteristics that will help you identify it. Technical terms were avoided in the descriptions. The few terms that are used are defined or shown in the Picture Glossary.

The descriptions contain a third type of information: the interesting human uses of each plant.

Many plants were used widely by the Paiutes and other southwestern Indians. Some were used by the Mormon settlers. These earlier inhabitants viewed the plants from the perspective of necessity; various species cured arthritis, fed hungry children, built barns and made rope. These facts about plants give us an insightful look at the earlier cultures and how they dealt with the land.

Remember, this is a basic guide to the showiest and most prominent plants of the Virgin Mountains. It covers only a fraction of the plant species found here. If the plants catch your interest, obtain one of the more comprehensive plant guides listed at the back of this booklet.

Picture Glossary

Technical terms were avoided when possible in the plant descriptions. In some cases, however, a single botanical term can replace a paragraph of descriptive, but non-technical words. When that was the case, the botanical term was used. The term was then defined in this glossary with a sketch or a short sentence.

Flowers

Parts of a Flower

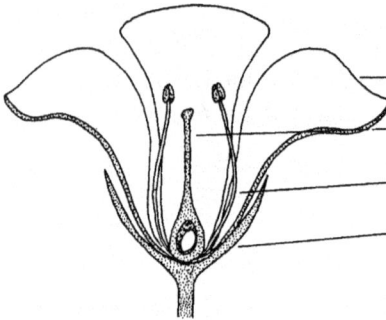

Flower With United Petals

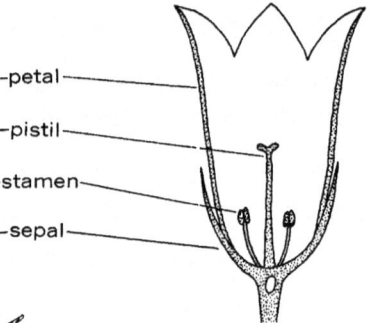

petal

pistil

stamen

sepal

Parts of a Pistil

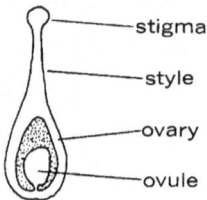

stigma

style

ovary

ovule

spike

Parts of a Stamen

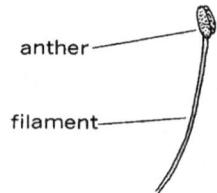

anther

filament

A Composite Flower Head

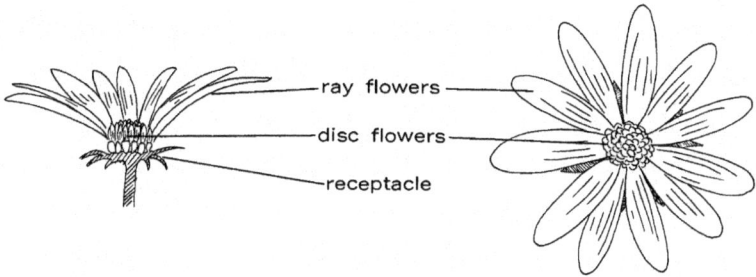

ray flowers
disc flowers
receptacle

Leaves

Leaf Shapes

pinnately-lobed   lanceolate shape   palmately-lobed   linear shape

Leaf Arrangement Along Stem

basal rosette   opposite leaves   alternate leaves   scale-like   needle-like
of leaves   leaves   leaves

Simple Leaves

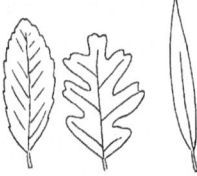

Compound Leaves

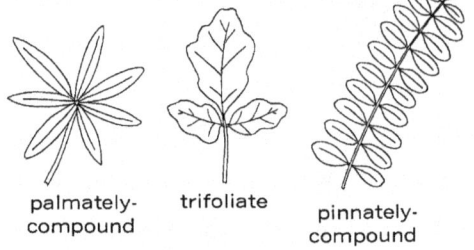

palmately-
compound

trifoliate

pinnately-
compound

Cactus Parts

Cholla Joint

Barrel Cactus
Tubercle

spine

areole

tubercle

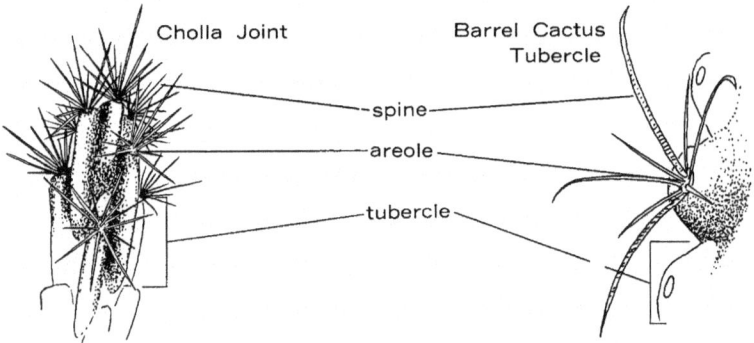

Some Useful Terms

Annual plant completes its life cycle in a single year.

Biennial plant completes its life cycle in 2 years; usually it remains a cluster of leaves during the first year, then sends up a flower stalk the second year.

Bilaterally symmetrical a flower that can be divided into 2 "mirror-image" halves (like the human face).

Deciduous leaves drop off as winter approaches or during prolonged drought.

Evergreen leaves remain on plant during cold or dry periods.

Herbaceous soft-stemmed plants which don't persist from year to year.

Node the point where a leaf or leaves emerge from the stem.

Perennial plant persists for more than one year, often flowering each year.

Succulent a plant which retains a high percentage of water in thick leaves.

Woody hard-stemmed plants (trees and shrubs) which persist from year to year.

The Meanings of Wildflowers

Flowers are used to express mankind's deepest emotions. They tell of our love; show sympathy for our sick; and express sorrow for our dead. Their brilliant colors and rapid growth from seemingly lifeless seeds express the exuberance and hope of the human spirit.

But flowers have quite another function in nature. Their bright colors and fantastic shapes evolved over millions of years for one purpose: pollination. In pollination, pollen fertilizes the female egg. From the fertilized egg, the seed develops; and from the seed, the young plant sprouts. Eventually, the growing plant produces flowers — and pollen — and the eternal cycle of life continues. Pollination, then, is a vital link in this cycle.

There are two basic ways for pollen to move from one plant to another: by wind and by animals. Wind-pollinated flowers have special adaptations allowing pollen to be caught by the wind and carried wherever the whim of the wind takes it — hopefully to another plant of the same kind. Of course, most of the pollen is wasted, so the flower has to produce prodigious quantities of the tiny pollen grains. To release the pollen, the flowers are specially made to dangle in the wind. The oak flowers in the drawing, for example, are built to dance around in the slightest breeze.

Most flowers in the desert, however, are built to attract animal pollinators. These include bats, hummingbirds, bees, flies, ants, butterflies, moths, and wasps. Generally, the flowers are made to appeal to one type of animal; a "hummingbird flower" is rarely visited by bees, and vice-versa. It is a sort of key-and-lock arrangement: the animal is the "key" that only fits a few kinds of flower "locks."

This specificity is accomplished by the flower's proficient use of color, shape, and smell. The fantastic rainbow of colors that attracts us to wild-flowers is not sensed by most other animals. Bees, for example, see only blue, yellow, and ultraviolet light; so they are attracted to flowers of those colors. Some flowers even have ultraviolet "colored" streaks and spots that guide bees into the flower (which, by the way, are invisible to us).

In contrast, hummingbirds are especially sensitive to red light, so flowers appealing to them are generally red.

This discussion of flower color brings up another point. Why is it that flowers are almost never green in color? The answer is obvious. Since the flower is trying to attract animals; it has to be brightly colored. Green would blend into the background of green foliage and be hard to see.

Flower shapes are often carefully fitted to the pollinator. Hummingbird flowers, for example, are often tubular in shape to accommodate their long beaks and tongues, and to discourage other insects who are not potential pollinators. They are generally projected outward, away from the plant, to accommodate the hummingbird's habit of hovering. Bee flowers, on the other hand, often have a projecting lower lip that serves as a bee landing pad; as well as a short, cave-like tube that bees have to force their way into to get the nectar.

Odors are used to attract animals such as bees, moths, and bats. When bees visit a scented flower, they pick up the scent and trail it through the air back to the hive. This smelly pathway shows the members of the hive how to get to the flower. Some of the strong-smelling, night-blooming flowers are designed to attract moths; who have strong senses of smell and good powers of distinguishing smells. Butterfly blossoms, in contrast, are only weakly scented, because butterflies have a poorly developed ability to sense smells.

A critical question remains: What's in it for the animal? Animals don't pollinate flowers as a free service. Actually, pollination is usually accidental from the animal's point of view. The animal seeks the flower's sugary nectar as food. After it drinks up the nectar of one flower, it moves to another flower; and another. At each step its body brushes against the flower's pollen-bearing stamens and accidentally picks up and carries away a load of pollen. Some of this pollen, by chance, is deposited on the next flower's stigma — and pollination occurs.

This generalized account doesn't give justice to the interesting array of inter-relationships between flowers and their pollinators. If you are mechanically-oriented, you'll enjoy figuring out exactly how the various flowers are built to ensure that visiting bugs leave with their load of pollen. These adaptations include colored guidelines, pools of nectar, false nectar, springs, traps, and brushes. After watching bees tumble around in a "trap" flower or be flung upside down by the floral equivalent of a coiled spring — you'll begin to think of flowers as miniature funhouses or amusement park rides.

But flowers are not designed for the amusement of either bees or people. They are designed for the very real energy requirements of animals — and for the necessity of plants to reproduce. Whatever pleasures we derive from looking at flowers, their original meaning lies in the functional relationships they have with animals.

As humans, however, we value wildflowers in several ways. For one thing, they have practical uses. Rockhounds, for example, can learn to associate certain wildflowers with certain rock formations. Hikers can roughly guess their elevation by the flowers they find. Fishermen can tell by the flowers if the season has progressed too far for good fishing. People lost in the wilds can use many plants as survival foods.

Wildflowers are also valuable to us in a historical and cultural sense. They accompanied our ancestors to their graves for thousands of years. Wild plants fed our predecessors; clothed them; provided them with medicines, and with shelter. Today, wild plants have a cultural value similar to books or museums or national parks. They are considered one of those "finer things" that make life worth living. So many people now live in the cities, where they rarely experience anything wilder than a potted geranium. Wildflowers, to them, have become a reassuring contact with the natural world. Like old friends...

Photographing Wildflowers

Flower photography poses problems unrelated to landscape or "people" photography. To take good photographs, you need to use special techniques and equipment. Here are some suggestions based on the experience of many flower photographers.

GET CLOSE!

Fields filled with flowers are rare in the desert. More often, the flowers are scattered, small, and difficult to photograph. For most, only close-up photography can reveal the textures and pure, undiluted colors you see when you look closely at a flower.

For many cameras, close-up lenses are available that can be attached in front of the regular lens. The best camera to use for flower photographs is the single lens reflex (S.L.R.) type. With this camera, you can add other types of close-up attachments such as extension tubes, bellows, and macro lenses; all of which allow ultra close-ups of flowers, leaves, insects, and whatever other small objects catch your eye. Additionally, when you look through an S.L.R.'s viewfinder, what you see is what is recorded on the film. That gives you good control over composition, focusing, and exposure; all of which are critical in fine flower photography. [ed. note: Now, of course, digital, rather than film photography is the norm.]

DEPTH OF FIELD

Most of the best flower close-ups are sharp, clear images that have the whole flower in focus. You can get good results by using the smallest diaphragm (f-stop) opening your camera lens allows. On most 35mm cameras, this is an f-16 opening. Unfortunately, when you close down the opening to get a good depth of field, you have to increase the exposure time to compensate. This is a problem if the wind is blowing.

TAMING THE WIND PROBLEM

Flowers dance in the wind. This is fine for motion pictures; but disastrous for still photography. On a really windy day, you might as well, forget about photographing flowers; the bad results aren't worth the time and effort.

You can avoid the wind problem on most days by going out early in the morning while the air is still. If there is a gentle breeze, have your companion stand where he or she blocks out most of the wind. Some photographers even "tie down" flowers with thread to subdue wind movements.

Body movement can also blur close-ups. A miniature tripod, a sandbag, or even a nearby rock will help steady your camera. A cable release will prevent jiggling when you actually take the picture.

KEEP THE BACKGROUND UNCLUTTERED

Flower photographs are more dramatic if the flower is bright and the background dark and uncluttered. Sometimes this happens naturally, but often you have to create your own dark background. Have a friend (or a rock) stand so a shadow is cast on the background, but not on the flower. Or, take a piece of dark cloth (or a pant-leg), and have it held behind the flower. The short depth of field will obscure the cloth's texture, yielding a nice, even background. This technique, however, lends a boring "sameness" to your pictures if used too often. Try to use an uncluttered, natural background whenever possible.

LOOK FOR THE UNUSUAL

A tiny blue butterfly, a yellow crab spider, an unusual shadow, glistening raindrops, morning dew . . . All these "little things" can make the difference between an ordinary and a prizewinning photograph. To achieve unusual effects, experiment! Try different times of day; the "red" light of early morning and evening creates interesting variations in flower color. Try different weather conditions; an overcast day often brings out brighter, more saturated colors than a sunny day. Try a rainy day; beaded raindrops covering a cactus blossom are unusual enough to capture attention. And finally, try discarding the flower photography "rules" discussed previously; use a short depth of field to throw all but one part of the flower out of focus. Or photograph in the wind to get a pleasing blur of colors. Some of the best flower photographs go against the prevailing "common sense" of flower photography.

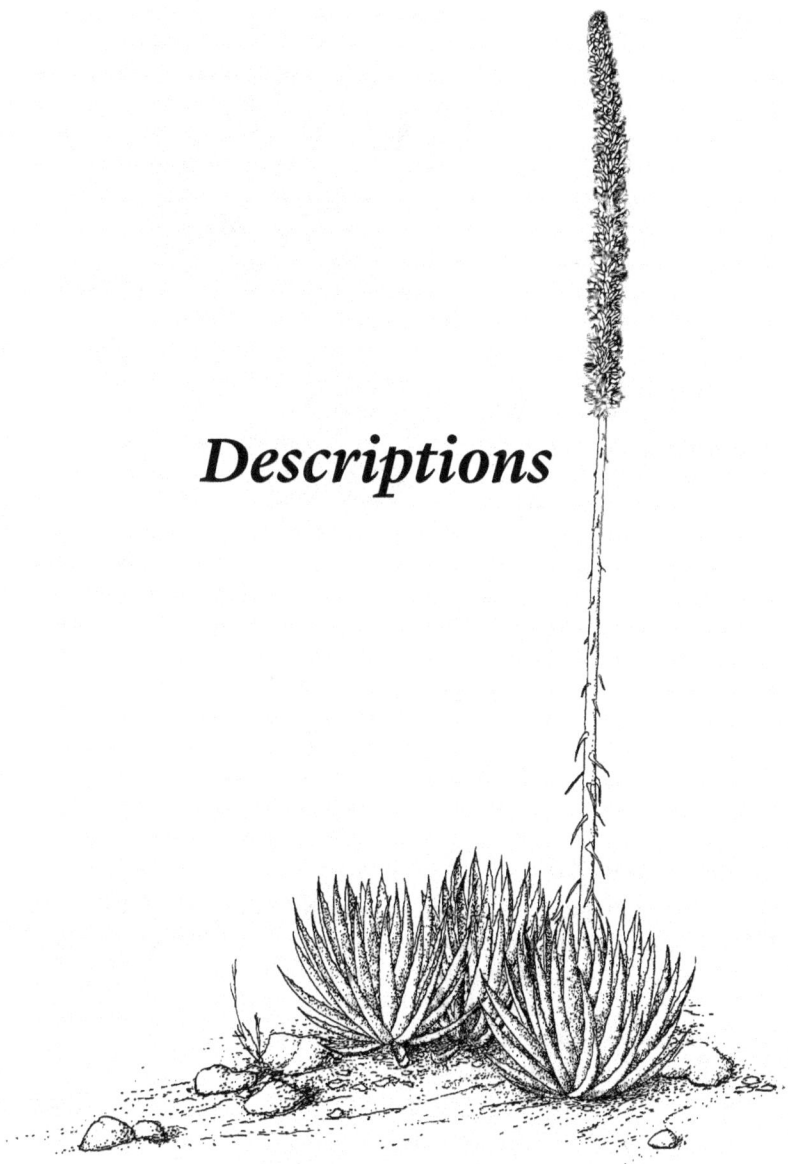

Descriptions

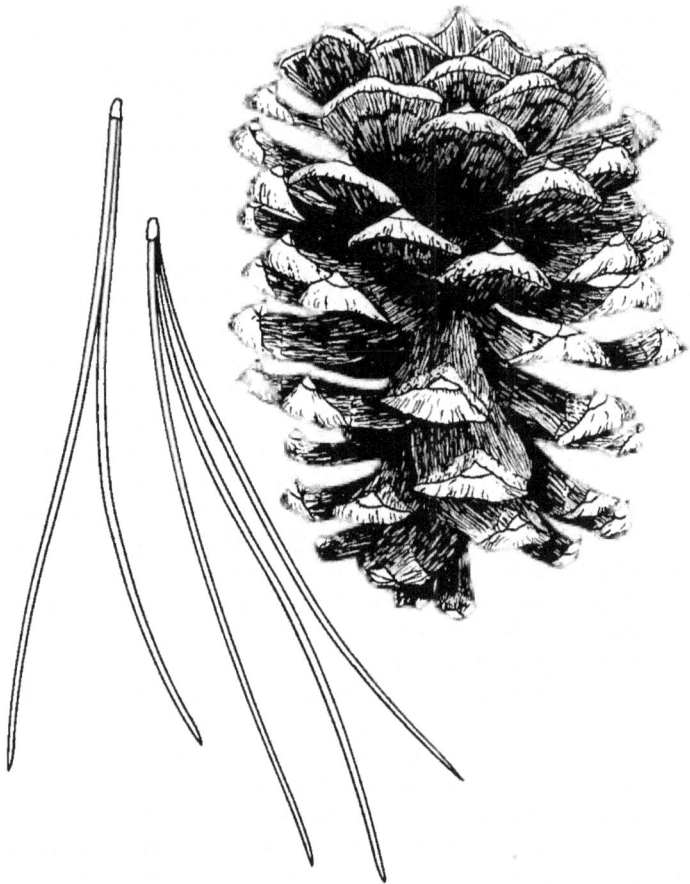

PONDEROSA PINE

Early Mormon pioneers cut and hauled ponderosa pines from nearby Mt. Trumbull to St. George along the Temple Trail. These were used in building the St. George Temple. Ponderosa pines are big trees, averaging 70 feet tall and 2 feet thick in the Virgin Mountains. They grow at elevations above 5500 feet, and form beautiful, park-like stands along the Virgin Ridge. They have clusters of 4-6 inch long needles with 2 or 3 needles per clusters. They smell like turpentine when crushed. The bark is dark and deeply-ridged in young trees, but with age it breaks into cinnamon-orange plates separated by dark fissures. The cones are 3-5 inches long and are armed with a deciduous prickle.

Pinus ponderosa   PINE FAMILY

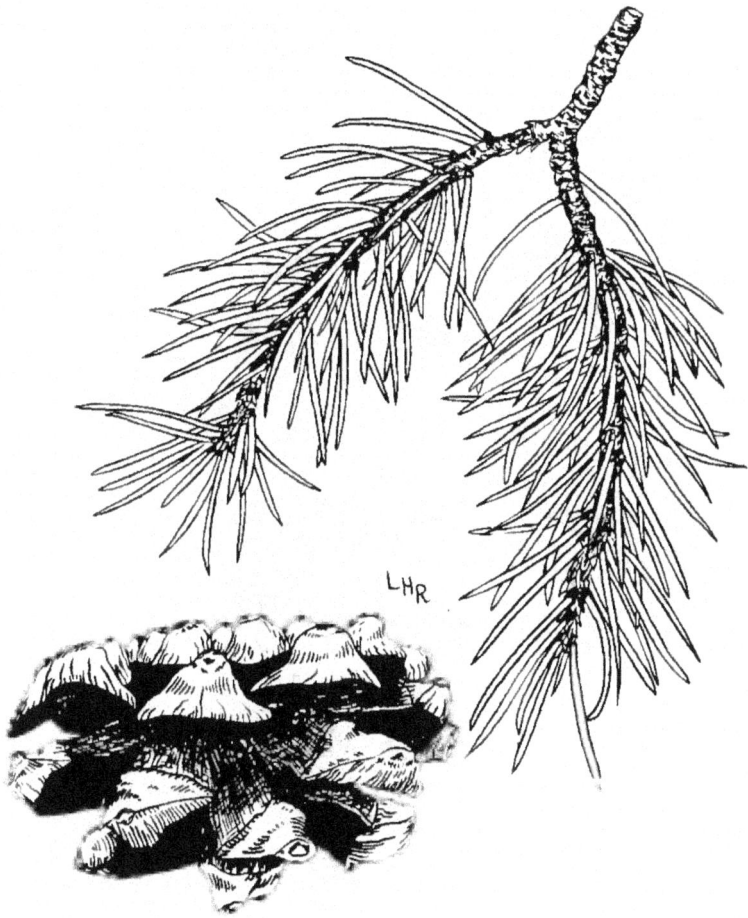

PINYON PINE

At 3000 calories per pound, pinyon pine nuts are one of those very rich, very fattening — but very good foods. They were a staple in the diets of early desert dwellers who journeyed many miles to harvest the autumn crop. Singleleaf pinyon usually grows as a twisted, 20-40 foot-tall tree. It has a small, rounded cone and the needles are single rather than clustered. With Utah juniper, pinyon pine forms the extensive "pygmy forest" clothing the Virgin Mountains between 4000 and 6500 feet. The pine nuts are especially good when roasted. To bring out their flavor, shake them in a hot pan over an open fire.

Pinus monophylla PINE FAMILY

DOUGLAS FIR

Tucked away on the north-facing slopes west of the Virgin Ridge, a little island of Douglas firs subsist on the rains and snows snagged by Mt. Bangs. Douglas fir is easily recognized by its 2–4 inches hanging cones, which have 3-lobed bracts sticking out from between the scales. The slightly flattened needles are long, evergreen, and grooved on their upper surface. The distinctive bud is shiny and shaped like a cone. The Douglas fir trees here are small and were apparently never used historically, but elsewhere in the West, they make up 50 percent of the standing timber and are harvested to make common plywood.

Pseudotsuga menziesii   PINE FAMILY

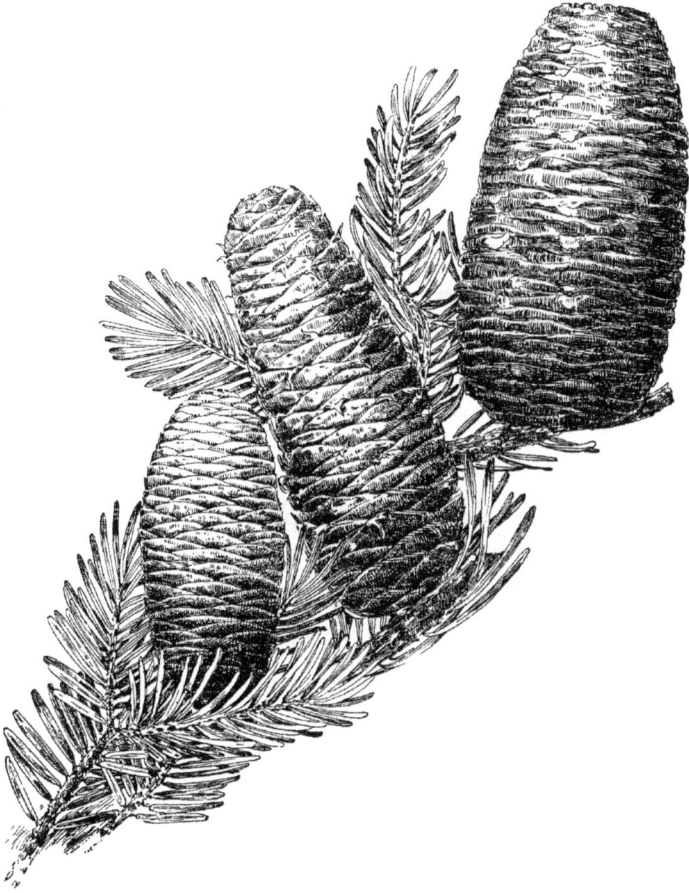

WHITE FIR

White fir grows with Douglas fir in isolated pockets high in the Virgin Mountains. The trees here are small and not commercially used. Elsewhere, they are planted ornamentally and sometimes used for a rough grade of inferior lumber. White fir's 3–5 inch cones stick upward, like candles, from the branches. They are olive-greenish to purplish, with deciduous scales. The 2–3 inch blunt-tipped needles are silvery blue/green and when pulled out of a twig, they leave shallow, rounded depressions in the twig's surface. Young trees have smooth, gray bark covered with little resin-filled bumps, while the bark of older trees becomes dark and deeply furrowed.

Abies concolor   PINE FAMILY

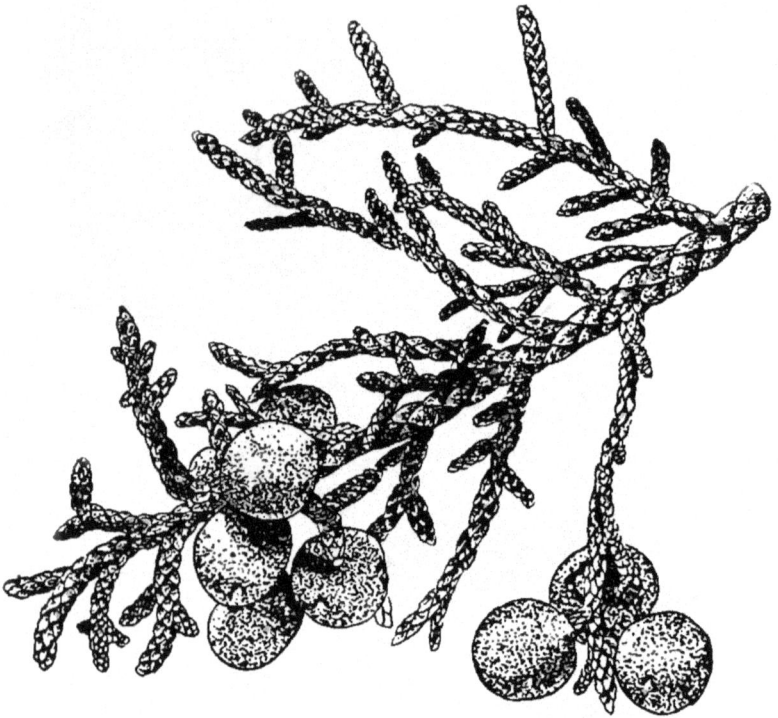

UTAH JUNIPER

The Utah juniper, together with pinyon pine, forms the pygmy forest occupying the belt between 4000 and 7000 feet in the Virgin Mountains. This small tree often has several main trunks arising from the same root system. The leaves are small, evergreen, scale-like, and lie closely pressed against the twig. The fruit is berry-like; 1/4–1/2 inch in diameter with a surface dusting of silvery-blue. In the past, Indians ground and formed the sweet (and resinous) tasting fruits into cakes. Ashes were used as a red dye and as a mordant for wool. Today, juniper is often considered a weed tree and is removed to make way for better cattle forage.

Juniperus osteosperma   CYPRESS FAMILY

MORMON TEA

Mormon tea is a 2–4 foot shrub growing in dry, open areas from the desert up through the pinyon-juniper belt. This plant is a mass of green, grayish, or yellowish stems. The leaves have been reduced to tiny opposite or whorled scales found at each node along the stem. The fruit is a small cone, actually closely related to the cones of pines and firs. Mormon tea was named for its use by Mormon settlers, who, because of a religious taboo, would not drink coffee or tea. The hot or iced tea (made from the dried stems by steeping 5 minutes in boiling water) is a very good desert thirst-quencher (note: no longer recommended due to possible adverse health effects).

Ephedra spp.   MORMON-TEA FAMILY

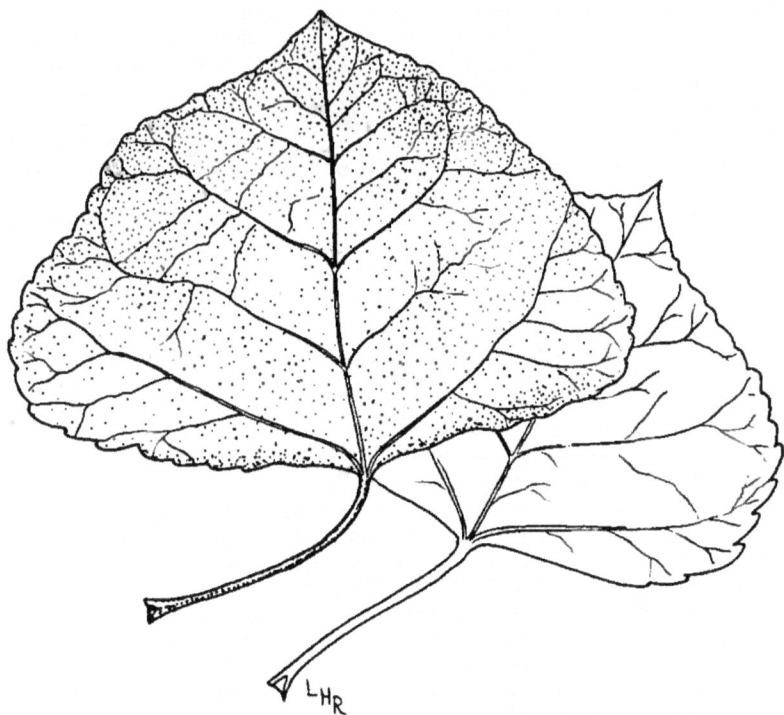

FREMONT COTTONWOOD

In July, when the sun sears the hot desert sands, Fremont cottonwoods still provide their fluttering, leafy shade. 50 foot tall specimens are found standing next to many springs in the Virgin Mountains. The leaves, borne on long petioles, are deltoid-shaped with shallow, rounded teeth on the edges. The fruits are catkins, each composed of many pods, which in turn contain many seeds. The tiny seeds are swept aloft when the wind fills their cottony "sails." Fremont cottonwood produces an inferior wood, but it was used by desert settlers as a readily available building material. Pima Indians ate the raw catkins as a vegetable and the sweet inner bark as an emergency food.

Populus deltoides subsp. *fremontii*   WILLOW FAMILY

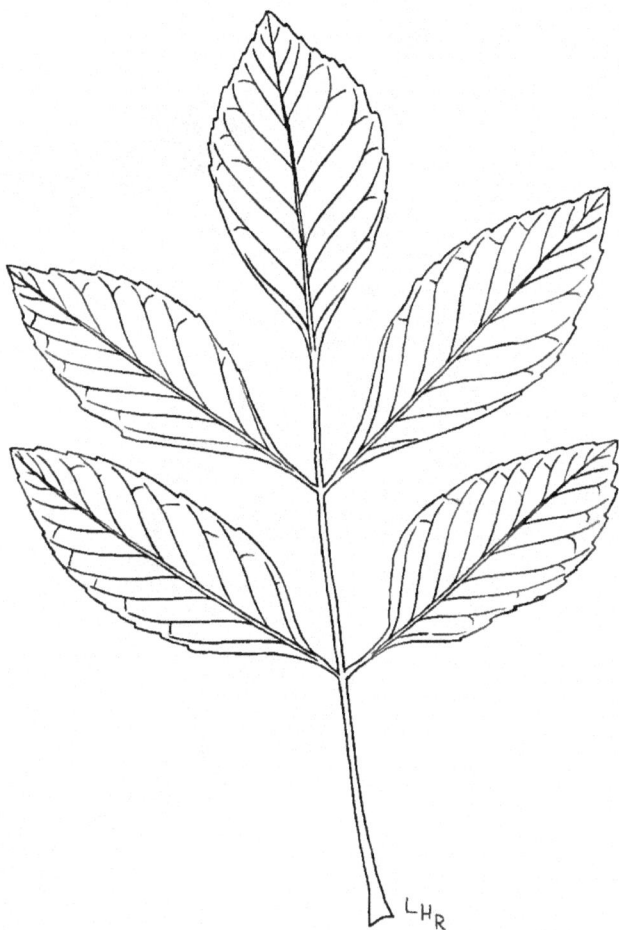

ARIZONA ASH

On a hot summer day, pass the afternoon in natural, air-conditioned comfort. Sit in the shade of an Arizona ash tree! These short (to 40 feet) trees are found near the campground along the Virgin River. This is a typical habitat; they grow well in riverbeds and washes at lower elevations. Arizona ash's leaves are opposite and pinnately compound, with 3 to 7 toothed leaflets. The seeds are borne in papery, winged fruits spread by the wind. Arizona ashes have been widely planted in southern Arizona as shade trees. Otherwise, they are not economically important and their pollen may cause spring hay fever.

Fraxinus velutina var. *glabra*   OLIVE FAMILY

SHRUB LIVE OAK

Shrub live oak is a shrub or small tree best identified by its holly-like, simple leaves that remain on the plant all year. These thick, leathery leaves are about 1 inch long, grayish-green, and spine-tipped. The acorns are 1/2– 1 inch long and are eaten by deer, squirrels, and an assortment of birds. Shrub live oak is found in open brushlands and in the pinyon-juniper belt. Indians of the southwestern deserts still use the ground acorn meats for bread and a marvelous acorn stew. Sometimes you'll find little, apple-like growths on oak leaves. These aren't a "normal" part of the plant. Instead, they are growths (called "galls") stimulated by tiny oak gall wasps.

Quercus turbinella   OAK FAMILY

GAMBEL OAK

Between 5000 and 8000 feet, Gambel oak trees stand huddled together in small clumps. These short, 20-foot trees are deciduous. Their dry leaves blanket the moist soil beneath the living trees; gradually decaying and enriching the earth with organic matter. The leaves are 2–4 inches long, with deep, narrow, rounded lobes. The inconspicuous early spring flowers are borne on dangling spikes. The hard, dense wood provided early settlers with fuel and fenceposts. The leaves are consumed by range cattle, but if eaten exclusively, they will kill the animals through kidney poisoning.

Quercus gambelii   OAK FAMILY

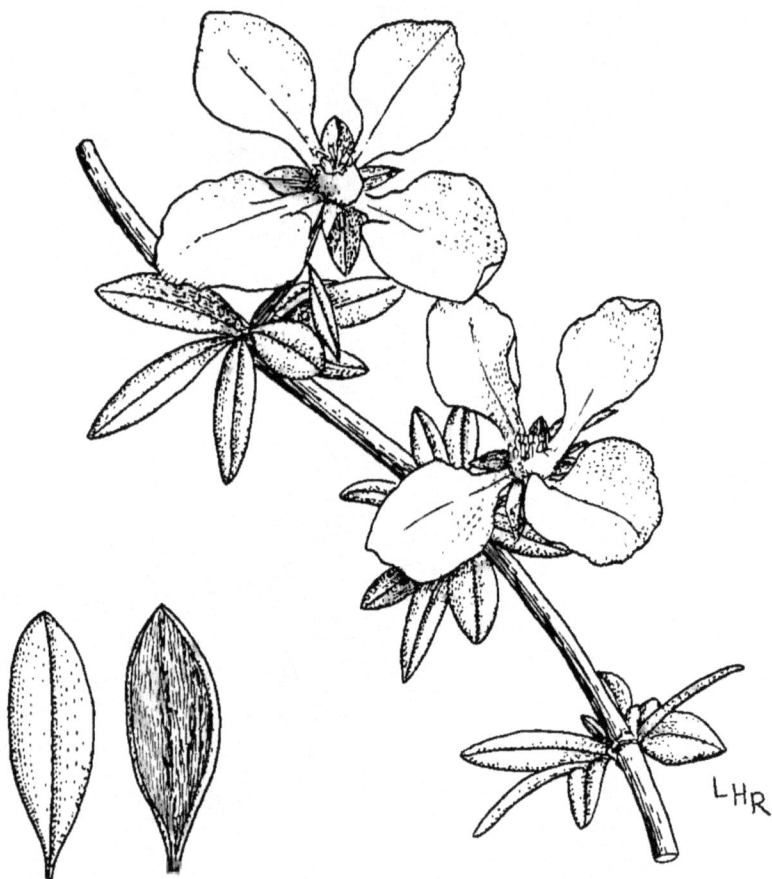

CLIFF FENDLERBUSH

Too many of our beautiful native flowers remain unknown to all but a few wildflower enthusiasts. Cliff fendlerbush is a good example. Its fragrant white flower would be a beautiful addition to home gardens, but so far, the plant has remained obscure, This 3–6 foot shrub grows on dry, rocky hillsides from 4000 to 7000 feet. The 1 to 1-1/2 inch flowers, blooming from April through June, have four spoon-shaped petals. The 3/4 inch long, thick leaves are opposite, linear, and have curled-under edges. The twigs are marked longitudinally by fine, white lines. Cliff fendlerbush is grazed by deer and by desert bighorn sheep (in their remaining ranges).

Fendlera rupicola   HYDRANGEA FAMILY

APACHEPLUME

   With a bit of imagination, apacheplume's seed clusters look like the war
bonnets of Apache warriors—hence the name. Apache plume is a bushy,
3–6 foot, white-barked shrub bearing cottony seed clusters in summer and
fall. The 1–2 inch, rose-like, April to June-blooming white flowers have 5
petals, numerous stamens, and are borne on long stalks. The small,
evergreen leaves are pinnately lobed. Apacheplume grows in dry washes
and on open rocky hillsides from 3000 to 8000 feet. The Hopis used this
plant to stimulate hair growth; while the Tewis used it to make arrow shafts
and brooms.

Fallugia paradoxa   ROSE FAMILY

MORTONIA

The thick, leathery, evergreen leaves of Mortonia create a strong geometric pattern up and down the branch. They are about ½" long, alternate, light green, and covered with minute bumps. The entire bush grows to 4 feet tall, with many stiffly upright branches. The flower is small, whitish, 5-parted, and blooms in April and May. Mortonia is common in lower Sullivan's Canyon and Migrant's Cove.

Mortonia utahensis   BITTERSWEET FAMILY

ROCK NETTLE

Rock nettle, also known as "stingbush", defends itself well with barbed, stinging bristles capable of chemically irritating a person's skin. A plant of the hot desert ranges, rock nettle grows at elevations to 3000 feet, usually in canyons or washes. Although it often grows as a 1-2 feet high, rounded shrub, it is more frequently found growing from cracks in rock faces. In the Virgin Mountains, rock nettle is conspicuous at the lower end of Sullivan's Canyon. The showy, 1-1/2 to 2 inch long, cream-colored flowers bloom from April to June. The bristle-covered, 1-2 inch leaves are broadly ovate and coarsely toothed.

Eucnide urens   BLAZINGSTAR FAMILY

CLIFFROSE

When temperatures are rising and the desert slopes seem dry and dusty, cliffrose bursts into its creamy-yellow flowers. This 3–12 foot, evergreen shrub grows from 4000 to 8000 feet on dry, rocky slopes. The 3/4 inch flowers with 5 petals and numerous stamens bloom between April and July, depending on elevation. The deeply lobed 1/4–1 inch leaves are covered with minute white hairs on the underside. The fruit has a feathery, 2 inch long tail. Great Basin Indians used the silky inner bark for cloth, mats, and ropes. Cliffrose is a valuable winter forage plant for cattle, but people find the twigs so bitter they've labeled it "quinine bush." Formerly classified as *Cowania mexicana*.

Purshia mexicana   ROSE FAMILY

LHR

DIXIE BLACKBRUSH

Perhaps blackbrush should be called the "plant of gloom," because it makes the landscape seem strangely dark even on a bright day. Blackbrush sometimes dominates the gravelly slopes and mesas from 3000 to 5000 feet, while elsewhere it grows with Joshua tree or Utah juniper. This 1–4 foot high shrub has numerous stubby, spine-tipped branches with opposite, crowded, leathery leaves. The yellow April and May-blooming flowers have 4 yellow sepals (functioning as petals), numerous stamens, and no actual petals. The flowers are located singly at the end of each branchlet. Although blackbrush provides fair winter cattle forage, some range managers would like to see it replaced with grasses.

Coleogyne ramosissima   ROSE FAMILY

CREOSOTE BUSH

If success is measured in numbers, creosote bush should be congratulated for its spectacular achievements. It covers vast areas of the southwestern deserts with its drab, avocado-green foliage. Named for its resinous odor, creosote bush is found on gravelly slopes in and around the Virgin River campground. Its many slender, 3–12 foot stems bear small, waxy leaves; each composed of 2 pointed leaflets. The 1 inch flowers, blooming in April and May, are bright yellow. They have 5 petals, each twisted like a propeller blade. The fruits are white and fuzzy "seed-balls." The Indians at Moapa, Nevada, used the red gum deposited on creosote bush stems by a lac insect for attaching tips to the shafts of mesquite-wood arrows.

Larrea tridentata   CREOSOTE BUSH FAMILY

SQUAWBUSH

What could be more refreshing than a tart, lemonade-like drink on a hot desert day? The berries of squawbush, crushed and soaked in water for 8 hours, then sweetened to taste, make a pleasant, pink "squaw-berryade." Squawbush is a deciduous shrub growing on hillsides between 2500 and 7500 feet. The small, yellow flowers emerge before the leaves. The bright green, shiny, aromatic leaves are usually trifoliate, but one variety has simple leaves. The 1/2–1 inch long leaflets have coarsely rounded lobes. The clusters of hairy berries are bright red and sticky. Indians boiled the foliage with pinyon pitch and yellow ochre to produce a black dye.

Rhus trilobata   SUMAC FAMILY

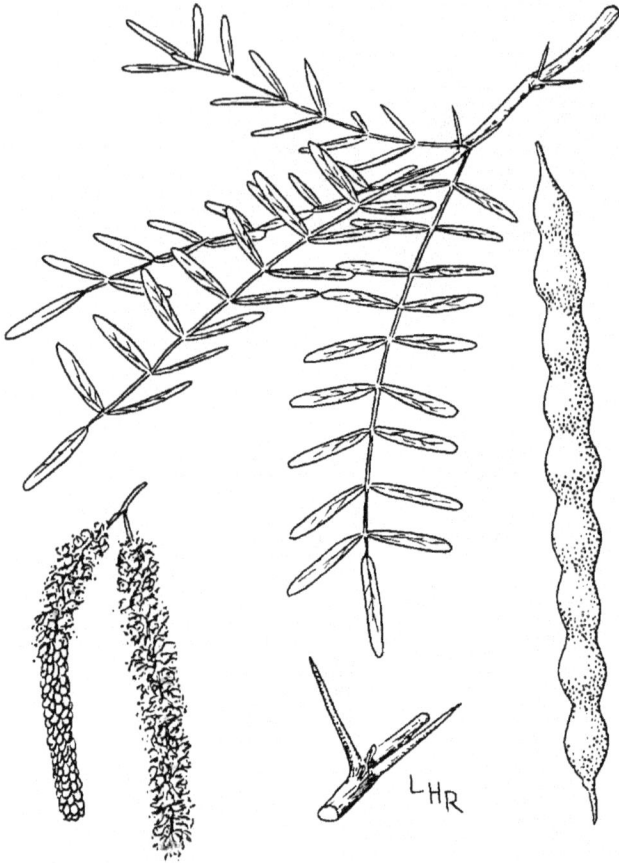

HONEY MESQUITE

Honey mesquite was a sort of wild "general store" to the early inhabitants who used it for food, fuel, drugs, candy, dye, basketry, hair coloring, liquor, diapers, pottery designs, skirts, and arrow tips. Mesquite is a thorny shrub growing to 30 feet tall in washes and low places below 5000 feet. Its pinnately compound leaves are composed of numerous small, green leaflets. The tiny yellow flowers bloom in May and June along 2-5 inches long, drooping spikes. Indians baked the 3-6 inch pods in the sun until they formed a solid, sugary cake. These cakes were used to make a meal called "pinole," which was in turn used by the Pima Indians to make an intoxicating drink.

Prosopis juliflora   PEA FAMILY

MANZANITA

When fire rages through a ponderosa pine forest, manzanita is among the first colonizers to revegetate the burnt landscape. It forms dense thickets, providing food and cover for a variety of animals, including deer. Manzanita, a beautiful, red-barked shrub, is too often considered a weed. The March/April flowers are 1/4 inch long, white with a pinkish base, and urn-shaped. The 3/4 x 1-1/2 inch leaves are thick and vary from shiny to hairy (depending on the species). The name "manzanita" is Spanish for "little apple." This is appropriate; the 1/4 inch diameter berries change in color from green to red, are edible (though mealy), and can be used to make cider and pie.

Arctostaphylos spp.   HEATH FAMILY
Arctostaphylos patula, Arctostaphylos pungens, Arctostaphylos pringlei

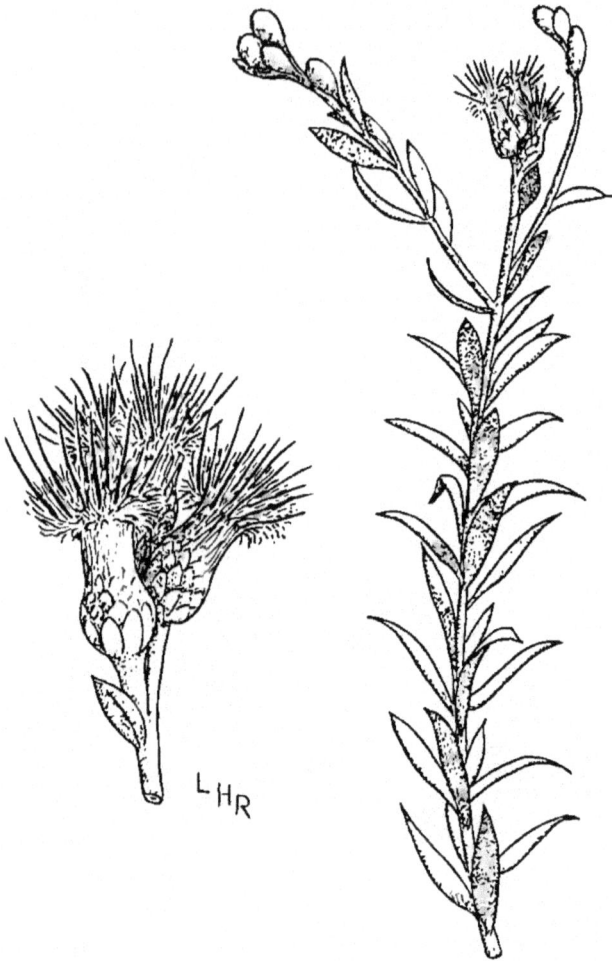

ARROW WEED

Like perfume, the foliage of arrowweed smells "nice" to some people; "rank" to others. Take your pick. This shrub with slender, straight, willow-like stems forms dense stands along river bottoms and around springs below 3000 feet. Its leaves are covered with silky hairs and appear silvery. The pale spring-blooming rose-purple flowers are found in clusters at the ends of the stems. Arrowweed was used by the Pima Indians for making arrow shafts, as well as for weaving baskets and building huts.

Pluchea sericea   ASTER FAMILY

TAMARISK

Along the Virgin River, the feathery foliage of tamarisk softens the hard edges of the desert. This is a looselybranched small tree or shrub growing to perhaps 25 feet tall. The deciduous leaves are tiny and scale-like. The pinkish-white flowers are also tiny and are borne along the ends of the slender branches. Tamarisk was introduced from the Mediterranean region in the 1800's. It escaped cultivation and now occupies river bottoms and dry washes throughout the West. It is highly drought-resistant, and although bees visiting tamarisk produce large quantities of honey, it is now considered a nuisance because it "drinks" tremendous quantities of scarce water.

Tamarix chinensis   TAMARISK FAMILY

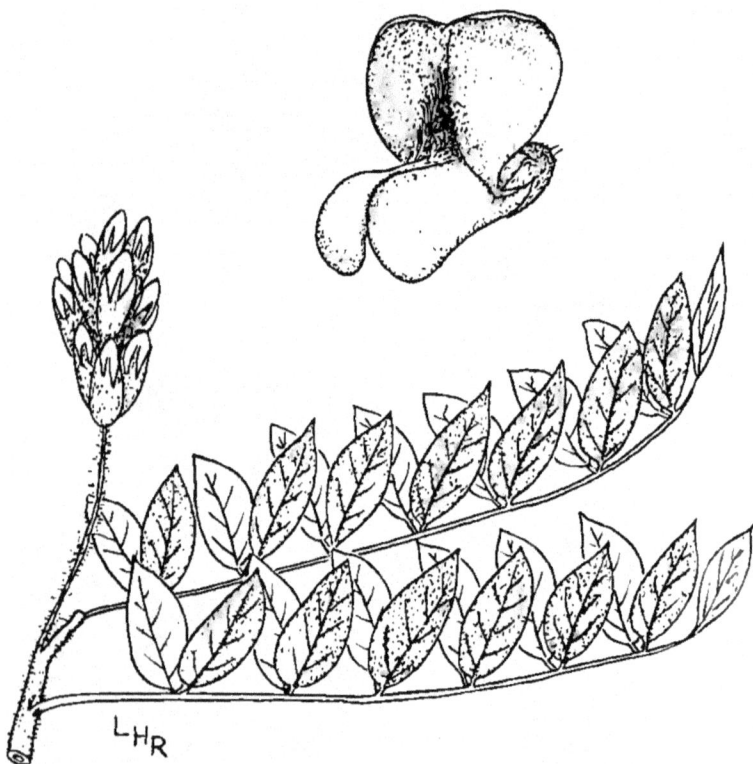

LHR

NEW MEXICAN LOCUST

Although the Hopi Indians used New Mexican locust to treat rheumatism, it is closely related to black locust — a notorious killer of children and livestock in the East. New Mexican locust is probably poisonous too. In canyon bottoms near 4000 feet, and on exposed places to 8000 feet, it is often found with Gambel oak and ponderosa pine. Commonly growing 10–15 feet tall, this shrub or small tree blooms May through July with showy clusters of fragrant, purplish-pink, pea-like flowers. The pinnately compound leaves have 9–21 large, rounded leaflets; while the legumes (seed pods) are covered with dense, bristly hairs. The wood makes excellent, naturally rot-resistant fenceposts.

Robinia neomexicana   PEA FAMILY

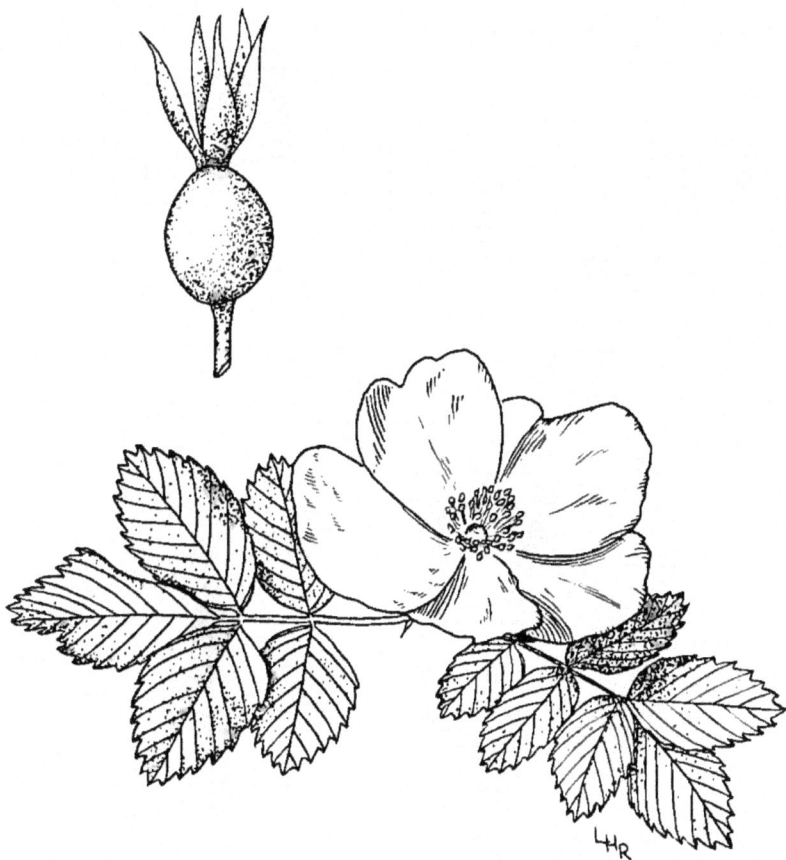

WILD ROSE

Lacking the refinements civilization has given its city cousin, the wild rose has retained a more austere, primitive beauty. Its 2 inch flowers, found near springs in the Virgin Mountains, have 5 pink petals surrounding the numerous stamens. The prickly stem bears alternate, pinnately compound leaves; each with 5–9 sharply toothed leaflets. The fruit is a bright red, berry-like "hip" maturing in autumn. While the hips are important to grouse and quail, they also provide people with an extremely rich source of vitamin C. Boiled rose hip pulp makes an excellent, fruity-tasting jelly. Raw rose petals add color and flavor to fresh salads.

Rosa spp.   ROSE FAMILY

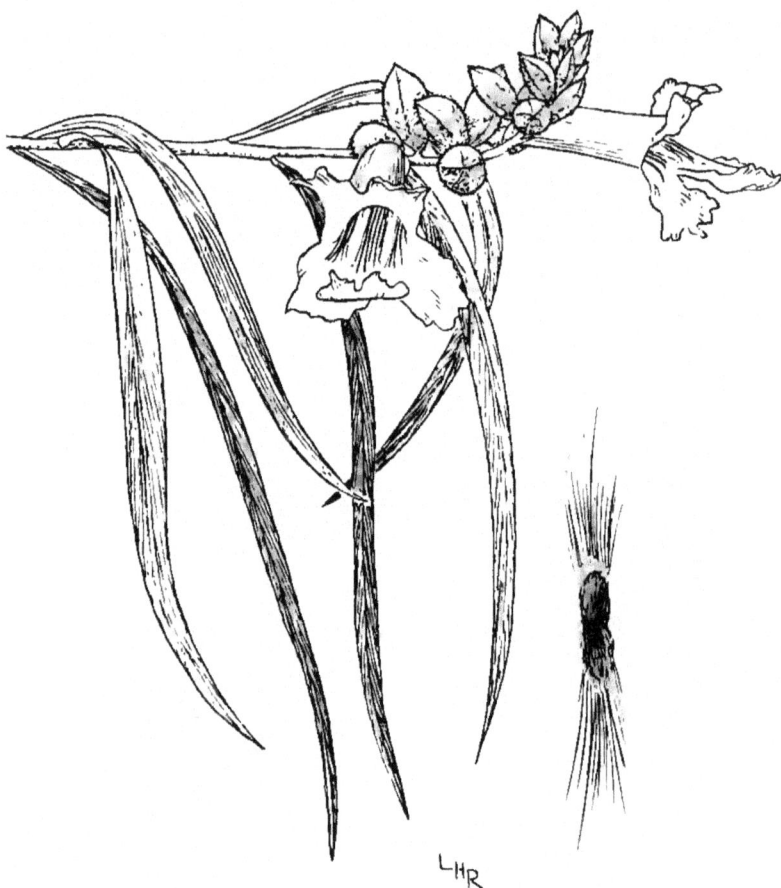

DESERT WILLOW

The desert willow sinks its thirsty roots into the dry washes of the
Mohave Desert. You'll find this small tree in Sullivan's Canyon, in the
series of canyons on the west side of the Virgin Mountains, and along the
Virgin River. After the willowlike leaves emerge in springtime, the desert
willow commences flowering and continues to flower through September.
The large (over 1 inch long) white to pink flowers are followed by the 6 inch
long seed pods which persist on the tree through the winter. The durable,
but twisted, trunks have been used for fenceposts, and the springy wood
provided Indians near Moapa with bows.

Chilopsis linearis   TRUMPET-CREEPER FAMILY

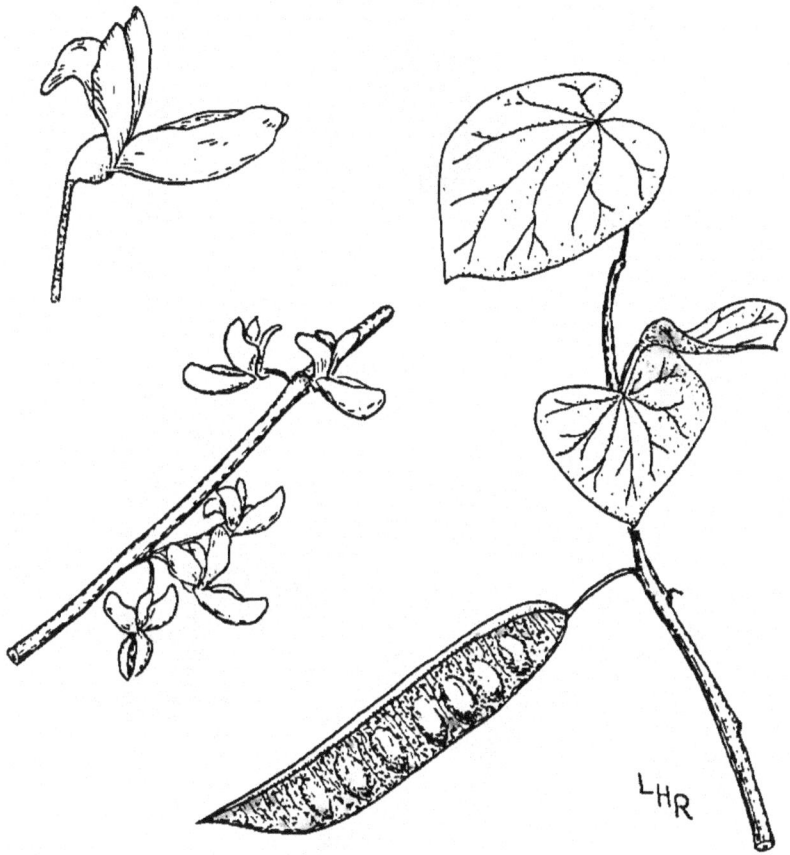

WESTERN REDBUD

Legends say that Judas, the disciple who betrayed Jesus Christ, hanged himself from a redbud tree. Ever since, redbuds (including western redbud) have been called "Judas trees". Western redbud's beautiful purplish-pink blossoms appear along old-growth twigs before the leaves emerge in the spring. After the flowers fade, the rounded, heart-shaped 2–4 inch leaves appear. Later, the 2–3 inch, pointed legumes (pods) mature. Western redbud grows on canyon slopes between 4000 and 4500 feet. The Porno and Yuki Indians of California used this small tree's bark for making baskets. The raw flowers can add color and a tangy flavor to contemporary salads.

Cercis occidentalis   PEA FAMILY

INDIGO BUSH

May brings the color of royalty to the desert. With its velvety, royal bluish purple flowers, indigo bush deserves its other name; "desert beauty." This thorny shrub has zigzag branchlets, supporting alternate, pinnately compound leaves with 1–7 oblong leaflets. It grows to 6 feet tall on dry slopes at elevations to 3000 feet. A related species was used by Moapa, Nevada, Indians to dye their basket willows yellow. Now sometimes classified as *Psorothamnus fremontii*.

Dalea fremontii   PEA FAMILY

JOSHUA TREE

A desperate group of early Mormons heading east toward Utah from California thought this tall, tortured yucca pointed the way to the promised land. They fittingly named it "Joshua tree". The bizarre forests of Joshua tree are found around the bases of Mohave Desert mountains where rainfall averages 8–10 inches per year. Joshua tree's May flowers are whitish and are borne on an 8–12 inch stalk. The flowers only appear in years when moisture and temperature are just right. When they do appear, they have to be pollinated by a specialized, night-flying yucca moth. The fine roots of Joshua tree were used by the Panamint Shoshones to create red and black patterns in their basketry.

Yucca brevifolia   CENTURY-PLANT FAMILY

BLUE YUCCA

Unlike most yuccas, which have leaves radiating from a short stem, the blue yucca's leaves emerge almost vertically from the ground. The 1-1/2 to 2-1/2 foot high leaves are gray-bluish-green and have coarse fibers peeling off the edges. A short flowering stalk (about as high as the leaves) bears 2–3 inch whitish blossoms between April and June. The blossoms are followed by large (to 6 inches), fleshy, smooth-skinned fruits that give this plant its other common name: banana yucca. Navajos enjoyed these fruits raw, roasted, and dried. Blue yucca's roots yielded a soap used for ceremonial hair-washings (and as a laxative).

Yucca baccata   CENTURY-PLANT FAMILY

UTAH YUCCA

Utah yucca defends itself with a delicate touch. Its narrow, rigid, very sharp-pointed leaves emerge from a 3-30 inch tall, aboveground stem. The 3-5 foot tall, many-branched flowering stalk blooms spectacularly in May and June with a large cluster of creamy-white flowers. The 1-1/2 inch long, 3-parted, woody capsules often remain on the old flowering stalk for several years. Utah yucca is found in the Migrant's Cove area of lower Sullivan's Canyon. Indians used yucca leaf fibers to make mats, rope, paintbrushes, and nets. During World War II, when the United States was short of jute fiber, a factory in Kingman, Arizona tried unsuccessfully to separate the fibers from yucca leaves.

Yucca elata   CENTURY-PLANT FAMILY

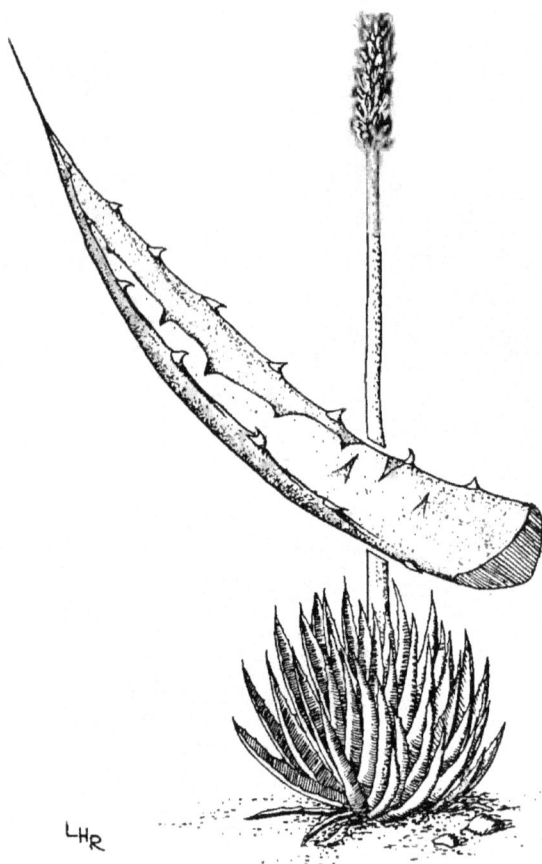

LHR

UTAH AGAVE

With a final burst of energy, Utah agave flowers after waiting its whole lifetime of 8–20 years; then it dies. The Paiutes harvested this final surge of energy by roasting (because raw agave is poisonous) and eating the emerging flower stalks; which tasted like sugary yams. They also fermented the agave pulp to make a primitive tequila. Utah agave grows singly or in clumps on rocky hillsides from 3000 to 7500 feet. The individual, 8–12 inch diameter "heads" are composed of thick, grayish leaves with hook-like spines along the edges (yuccas have smooth or fibrous edges). The flower stalks, rising 6–8 feet high and covered with 1 inch yellow flowers, look like candles rising from the cliffs.

Agave utahensis   CENTURY-PLANT FAMILY

SILVER OR GOLDEN CHOLLA

Silver cholla and golden cholla are one and the same species. The different names are given because of the genetically varied spine color, which gives the plant a silvery or golden "halo." The 2–6 inch long joints are shorter than those of the buckhorn cholla, as are the 1/4–1/2 inch long and 1/4 inch wide tubercles. The trunk is usually 1/3 to 1/2 the total height of the plant. Silver/golden cholla is found on gravelly or sandy slopes and flats below 3000'. The Pima Indians baked cholla flower buds overnight in deep pits by alternating cholla layers with hot stones. The baked vegetable was then dried. Now sometimes classified as *Cylindropuntia echinocarpa*.

Opuntia echinocarpa   CACTUS FAMILY

BARREL CACTUS

This "symbol of the desert" is abundant on the rocky cliffsides surrounding the Virgin River Canyon campground. When mature, barrel cacti average 1 foot thick and 2–3 feet high. The dense spines covering the ribs make the plant appear reddish or yellowish. The spines are paired, with the largest pair vertically oriented, irregularly curved, and 2–4 inches long. The large yellow May flowers are followed by sour-tasting, fleshy, yellow fruits that were eaten raw and made into cactus candy by early desert dwellers. The myth persists that barrel cacti are filled with cool, clear water. They aren't. The stem is actually filled with a moist, bitter pulp not worth the sweat lost in getting it out.

Ferocactus cylindraceus   CACTUS FAMILY

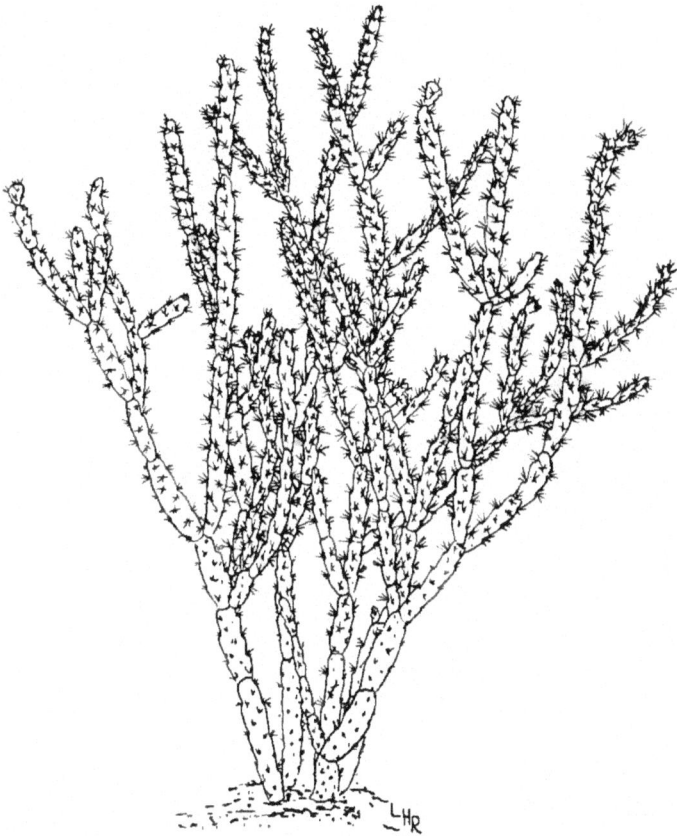

BUCKHORN CHOLLA

At least two cholla (pronounced "choy' yah") cacti are found around the base of the Virgin Mountains. These cacti average 4 feet tall and are many-branched, with each joint having a round (rather than flattened) cross section. Buckhorn cholla is the more common of the two. It has a very short trunk, or no trunk at all. The joints are 6–12 inches long, and the tubercles (see picture glossary) are elongate, 3/4 to 1-1/4 inches long, and 1/4" wide. There are about 15 straw-colored spines per cluster, and the clusters are widely spaced, enough that the predominant color is that of the green stem. Buckhorn chollas are found on dry, gravelly hillsides below 3500 feet; often mixed with creosote bush. Now sometimes classified as *Cylindropuntia echinocarpa*.

Opuntia acanthocarpa   CACTUS FAMILY

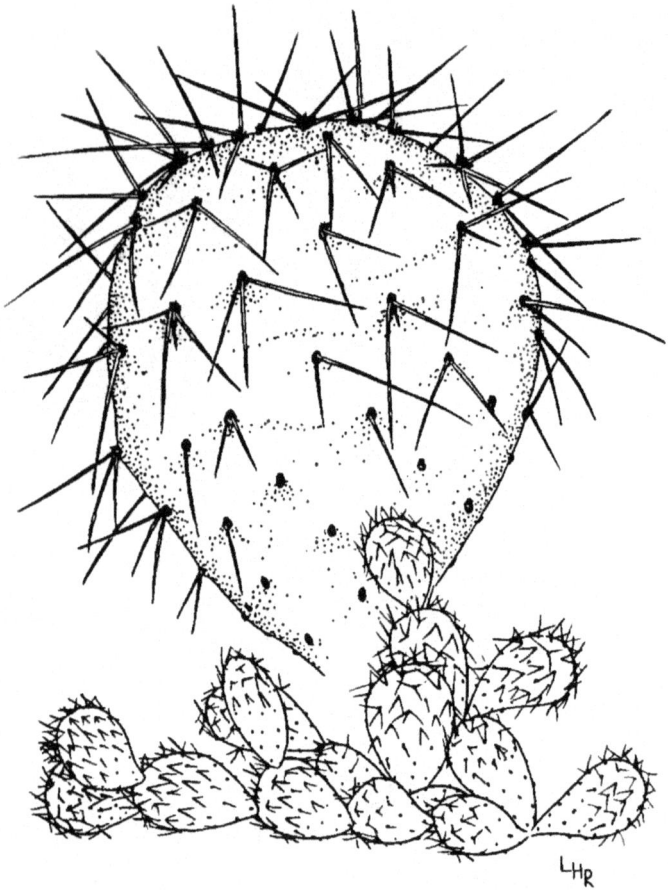

RUNNING OPUNTIA

Running opuntia forms chains of joints that run on edge in straight lines along the ground. This conspicuous cactus of the pinyon-juniper forest forms large clumps to 3 feet tall and perhaps 8 feet in diameter. The joints, or "pads" are 4-10 inches long and 2-1/2 to 6 inches wide. The 1-3 inch spines are concentrated toward the top 2/3 of each joint. The May/June, 2-1/2 to 3-1/4 inch diameter flowers are bright yellow. The pads are often eaten by jack-rabbits, while people eat the reddish-purple, fleshy fruits. These fruits, called "tunas" or "Indian figs," can be eaten raw, stewed, fried or boiled down to make syrup — but be careful, some Indians insist that eating too many tunas gives you chills.

Opuntia phaeacantha   CACTUS FAMILY

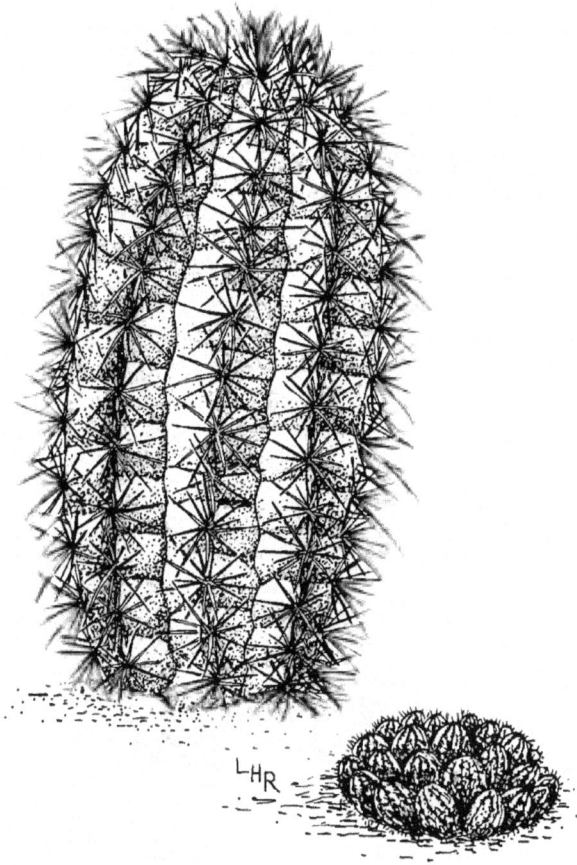

HEDGEHOG CACTUS

"Hedgehog cactus" accurately describes this plant; its spines are reminiscent of a European hedgehog's quills. The April to June blooming, clear scarlet flowers, called claret cups, are 1-1/4 to 2 inches in diameter. Hedgehog cactus grows in geometric mounds composed of a few — up to 500 — stems on rocky hillsides in pinyon-juniper and ponderosa pine woodlands. The cylindrical stems are 1-1/2 to 2-1/2 inches in diameter and 1-1/2 to 8 inches tall. There are usually 9 or 10 ribs and the tubercles can be seen. The light grayish spines rarely obscure the green stems. Like most cacti, hedgehog cactus is genetically extremely variable. The characteristics of flower size and shape, spine color, and number of spines can vary tremendously. Previously classified as *Echinocereus triglochidiatus.*

Echinocereus mojavensis   CACTUS FAMILY

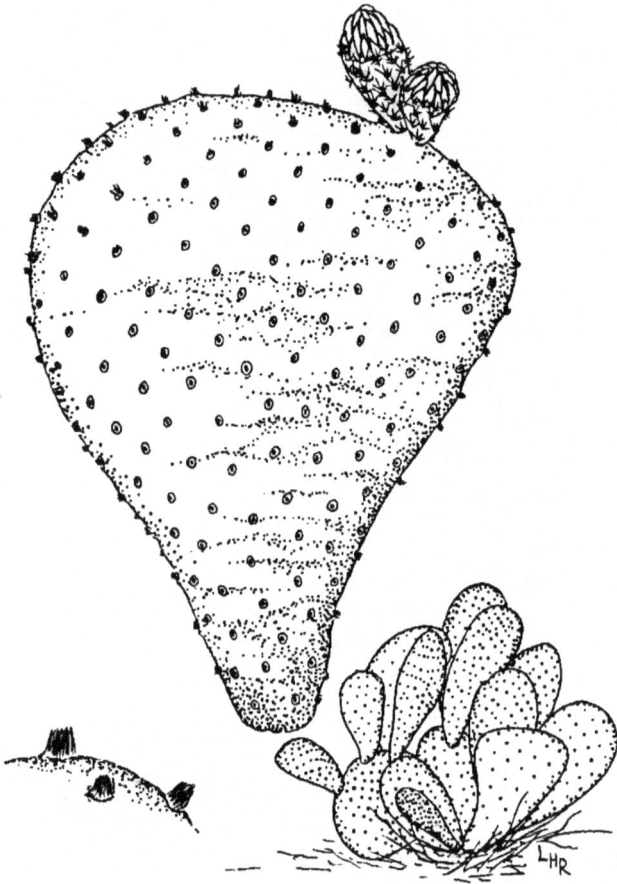

BEAVERTAIL CACTUS

Appearances can be deceptive. With its apparently spineless stems'and beautiful magenta blossoms, the beavertail cactus looks harmless. Don't believe it! Each "spineless" areole is actually a pit filled with hundreds of tiny, 1/8 inch long spines called glochids. A hint: if you get these spines in your finger, don't try to pick them out with your teeth — or you'll have glochids in your gums. Beavertail cactus grows in the lower areas of gravelly canyons to 3000 feet. The 4–12 inch joints grow in small clumps to 1-1/2 inches high. The Panamint Indians dried the joints and ate them salted and boiled during the winter.

Opuntia basilaris   CACTUS FAMILY

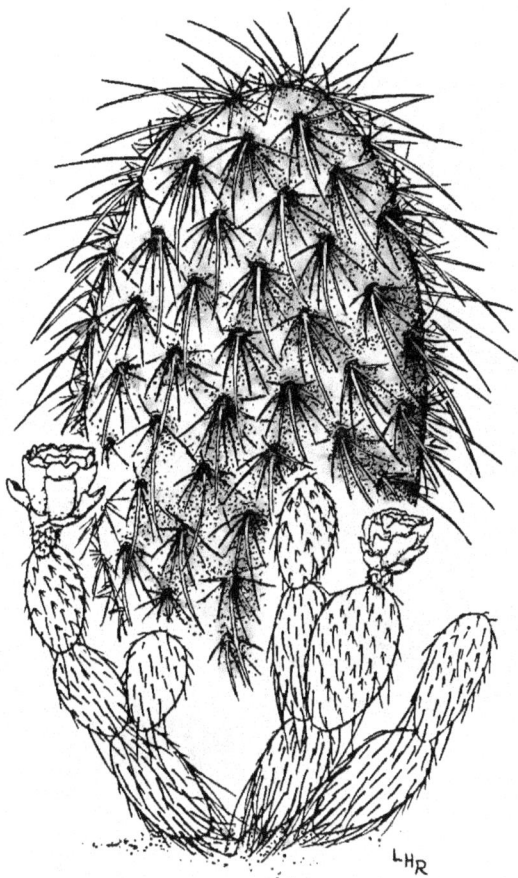

GRIZZLY BEAR CACTUS

Clumps of grizzly bear cactus brighten the rocky hillsides from April to June with their bright pink or yellow flowers. This cactus grows in clumps 1 to 1-1/2 inches high and up to 3 feet in diameter at elevations from 2500 to 4000 feet. The joints are pear-shaped; 3–6 inches long, 2 to 3-1/2 inches wide, and densely covered with whitish spines that some people compare to grizzly bear hair. The oldest joints, and the lower parts of younger joints, develop 3–8 inches long, thread-like spines. The fruits are dry, inedible, and densely spiny. During times of famine, desert Indians were forced to burn the spines off *Opuntia* pads and roast them for food.

Opuntia polyacantha var. *erinacea*   CACTUS FAMILY

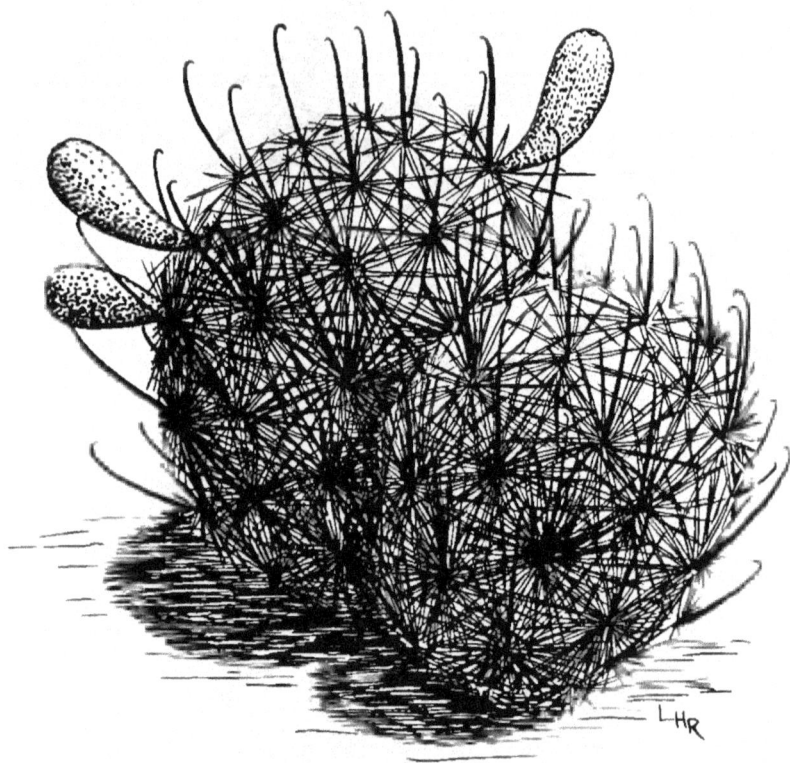

FISHHOOK CACTUS

This tiny cactus is easy to miss. It's only 2-6 inches tall and is often tucked in amongst the rocks of the low canyons and hillsides where it's found. Each cylindrical tubercle is nearly obscured by the 30-60 white lateral spines coming almost horizontally out of each areole. The really distinctive feature of fishhook cactus is the dark, hooked spines that emerge vertically from each areole. The rose-pink flowers are rarely seen, but the bright red, club-shaped fruits (called "lady fingers") often linger on the plant for a long time. The Shoshone Indians of Nevada collected and ate these fruits.

Mammillaria tetrancistra   CACTUS FAMILY

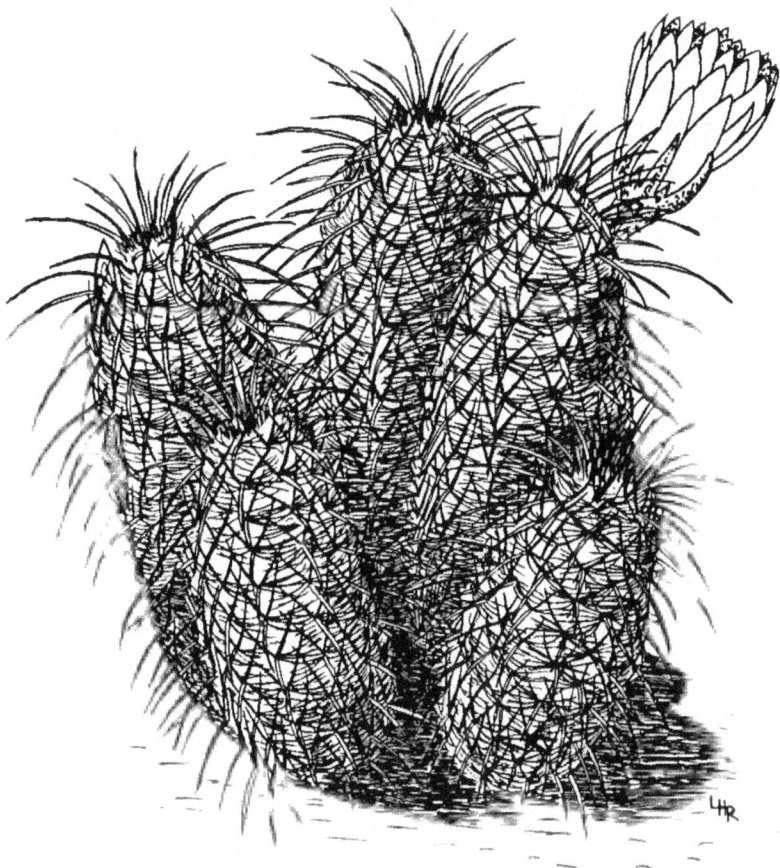

PURPLE TORCH CACTUS

The purple torch cactus is named for its showy purple flowers blooming in April and May. This plant grows as a cluster of 6–10" high, ribbed stems. Each cluster may have from 4 to 10 or more stems. The dense spines vary in color from whitish to yellowish to straw-colored to brown; the largest one is (usually) whitish and points downward. This "calico cactus" is found on rocky hillsides between 2000 and 5000 feet, often growing atop large rocks. You'll often see it growing near barrel cactus. The fruit is red, edible, and was relished by the Pima Indians.

Echinocereus engelmannii   CACTUS FAMILY

SEGO LILY

During the hard years of 1848 and 1849, frost, drought, and crickets ravaged the grainfields of the Mormon pioneers. Friendly Ute Indians taught the hungry settlers how to dig and eat sego lily bulbs, which reputedly saved many lives. The grateful people of Utah later named sego lily their state flower. Sego lily's 1-3 inch May to July flowers have 3 brilliant white (or lavender) petals; with dark maroon and yellow patches near the base of each petal. This 6-12 inch herbaceous perennial stores food and water in a deeply buried bulb. Sego lily is found in open pine forests and on slopes from 4500 to 8000 feet.

Calochortus nuttallii   LILY FAMILY

SLENDER WOODLAND STAR

In the dappled shade under aging ponderosa pines, the slender woodland star displays its frail, ephemeral blossoms. Sometimes the slender stem disappears into the shady background, leaving the sunlit flowers seemingly suspended like little stars. These small, attractive flowers are white or pinkish; they have 10 stamens and 5 deeply cleft petals. The divided leaves are highly variable; some lobes are broad, some narrow. All are palmately lobed. Slender woodland star, a perennial, grows from 4 to 20 inches tall at high elevations in the Virgin Mountains. Look for it near Mt. Bangs and atop Black Rock Mountain.

Lithophragma tenellum   SAXIFRAGE FAMILY

PRICKLY POPPY

"Look, but don't touch!" That's the message we get from prickly poppy. This herbaceous perennial has showy white flowers, but its leaves, buds, and 2–3 foot high stems are heavily armed with stout spines. The 3–4 inch diameter flowers are composed of 4–6 "wrinkly" petals surrounding a globe-shaped mass of yellow stamens. In the center of this mass is a large, dark stigma. Prickly poppy grows in dry, rocky areas and roadsides at low-desert elevations. The Shoshone and Paiute Indians used an alkaloid-containing tea made from the seeds as a strong purgative.

Argemone munita   POPPY FAMILY

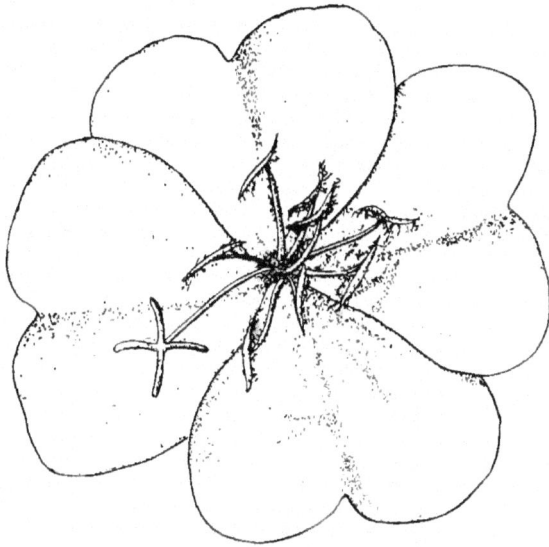

EVENING PRIMROSE

Evening primrose flowers work the night shift. By early morning they have finished their jobs and by noon they have withered and turned pink under the harsh sun. These 3–4 inch fragrant flowers attract night-flying insect pollinators. The flowers are stemless, with 4 white petals surrounding 8 stamens and a long stigma with 4 narrow lobes. The dense leaves are long, narrow, and shallowly lobed. White tufted evening primrose blooms from May through August on dry, rocky slopes from 4000 to 7500 feet. In the Virgin Mountains, it is found along the trail from the South Trailhead down to Atkin Spring.

Oenothera caespitosa   EVENING-PRIMROSE FAMILY

FRAGRANT SAND VERBENA

In the hot desert, where water is scarce and often tainted, Indians needed remedies for frequent kidney and bladder troubles. At Moapa, the Paiutes used a very close relative of fragrant sand verbena to treat these troubles. The fragrant sand verbena is an herbaceous, trailing plant with opposite leaves and white flowers. It grows to 12 inches long on the sandy floodplains of the Virgin River. There its sticky leaves frequently become covered with sand grains. The fragrant flowers, appearing in April and May, occur in clusters. Each flower in a cluster is a 1 inch long, slender tube with a crinkly, flared opening.

Abronia fragans   FOUR-O'CLOCK FAMILY

SACRED DATURA

Sacred datura is among the most conspicuous plants of the desert. Its many bright white, 6–8 inches long, trumpet-shaped flowers open in the evening to a diameter of 4–8 inches. The leaves are large (3–10 inches long), coarse, and rank smelling. The fruit is a prickly berry. The plant grows to a height of 2–3 feet in open areas below 4000 feet. You'll often see it along roadsides and in washes. Sacred datura was used ceremonially by the Indians at Moapa, Nevada, to induce hallucinations. It is dangerously poisonous, and consumption of its parts can lead through the beginning stage of insatiable thirst to the final stages of convulsions and coma.

Datura wrightii   NIGHTSHADE FAMILY

WATERCRESS

What is a European culinary delight like watercress doing in an obscure place like the Virgin Mountains? Growing ... wherever it can, in the soggy soil surrounding springs. The masses of watercress leaves are anchored to the mud by white roots sent out from nodes along the stem. Watercress has dark green, pinnately compound leaves, with 3–9 smooth-edged leaflets. The small, white, terminal clusters of flowers can be seen from April to August. Introduced from Europe, watercress spread over most of the United States. Its slightly bitter leaves are good raw in salads, but they never caught on widely here — too bad, for if the Romans were right, watercress is a cure for deranged minds.

Nasturtium officinale   MUSTARD FAMILY

FOOTHILL DEATHCAMAS

When Mormon pioneers first arrived in Utah, they gathered bulbs from several plant species for food. Sometimes they gathered, cooked, and ate deathcamas bulbs by mistake. This probably resulted in numerous tragic deaths. Cases of human poisoning still occur, and deathcamas is credited with being one of the most frequent sheep-killers, in the West. Foothill deathcamas is an herbaceous perennial growing between 5500 and 7500 feet; often associated with ponderosa pine. The leaves are grass-like, but are creased in a deep V along their length. The cream-colored May flowers, rising on a 3–12 inch stalk, are arranged in a terminal cluster. The fruit is a 3-lobed capsule. Now sometimes classified as *Toxicoscordion paniculatum*.

Zigadenus paniculatus   LILY FAMILY

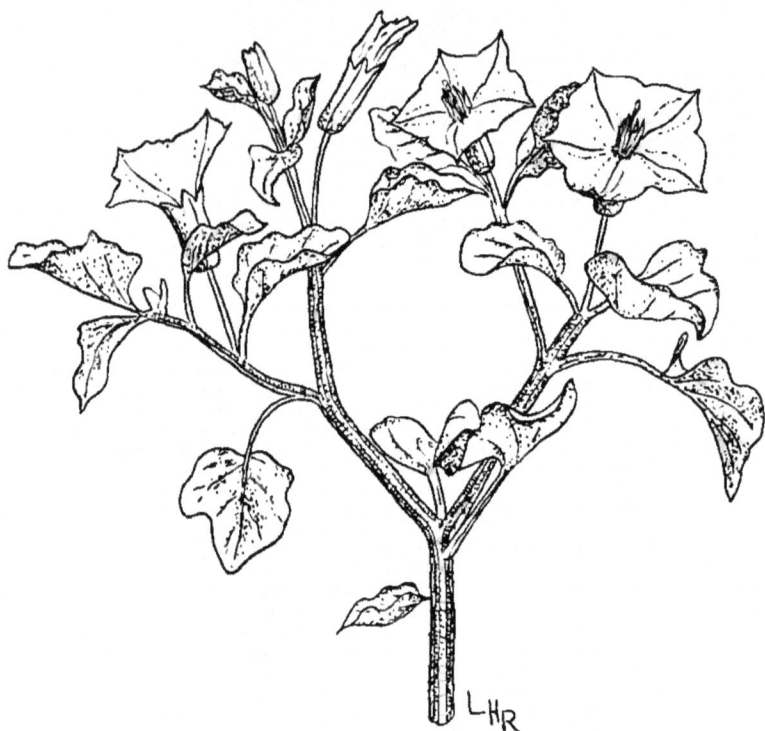

GROUND CHERRY

This member of the potato family is closely related to the Chinese Lantern plants so often planted in American gardens. The flower of the ground cherry is pale-yellow and about 1/2 inch across. Its petals are joined ! together (as in potato and tomato flowers). This species has a woody base and is adapted to grow under the desert conditions of dry, rocky slopes at lower elevations. The 1/2 inch diameter berry is enclosed in a papery green (to tan) husk. It is edible and was eaten by most desert Indians. Many contemporary foragers also enjoy the succulent berries on dry desert days.

Physalis crassifolia   NIGHTSHADE FAMILY

YELLOW DAY PRIMROSE

A variety of yellow day or evening primroses grow in the Virgin Mountains. All have 4 yellow petals and 8 stamens; but the flower size and foliage characteristics differ. Yellow day primrose, unlike most members of this group, flowers throughout the day. It is herbaceous, 8–30 inch tall, and has medium-sized flowers with petals up to 1/3 inch long. The pinnately compound leaves have irregularly shaped leaflets; the largest | one at the tip. Most of the leaves are concentrated at the plant's base, and they are often red-veined on the undersides. Yellow day primroses grow along the Virgin River and on rocky slopes of the low desert. Now sometimes classified as *Chylismia multijuga*.

Oenothera multijuga   EVENING-PRIMROSE FAMILY

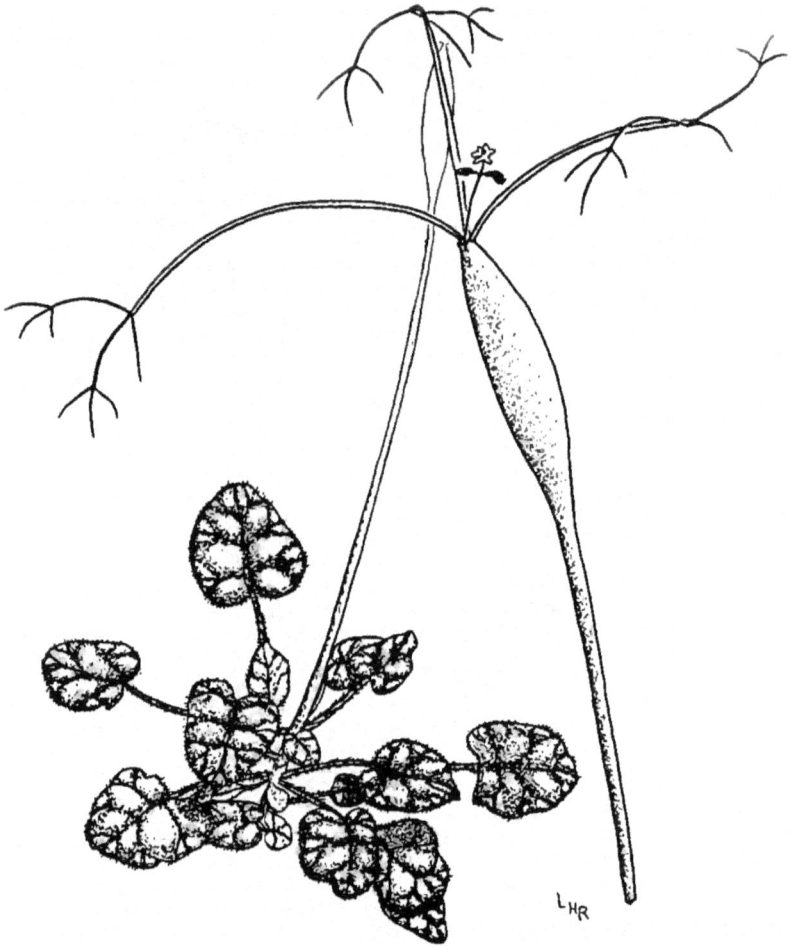

DESERT TRUMPET

This 8–30 inch high plant is easily recognized by its inflated stem (which divides into 3 parts just above the inflated section). The leaves are arranged in a basal rosette, while the tiny, inconspicuous yellowish green flowers are borne on thread-like stalks. Desert trumpet is found on rocky hillsides and gentle slopes below 6000 feet. This plant is also known as "Indian Pipe Weed." The Indians at Moapa used the hollow stems as pipes by placing a pinch of tobacco in the inflated section, and inhaling through the long tube.

Eriogonum inflatum   BUCKWHEAT FAMILY

PRINCESPLUME

Princesplume absorbs selenium, a mineral poisonous to cattle (and people), from alkaline, selenium-bearing soils of canyons and washes below 5000 feet. A perennial to 5 feet tall, princesplume sends up plumes of bright yellow flowers in May and June. The pistils extend out from the 1/2 inch long flowers, giving the flower "spikes" a fringed appearance. The flowers, each with 4 clawed petals, bloom in a wave along the spike, beginning at the bottom and progressing toward the top. The 2–8 inch leaves are grayish; the lower ones pinnately divided or compound. Death Valley Indians ate the specially prepared leaves as "Paiute Cabbage."

Stanleya pinnata   MUSTARD FAMILY

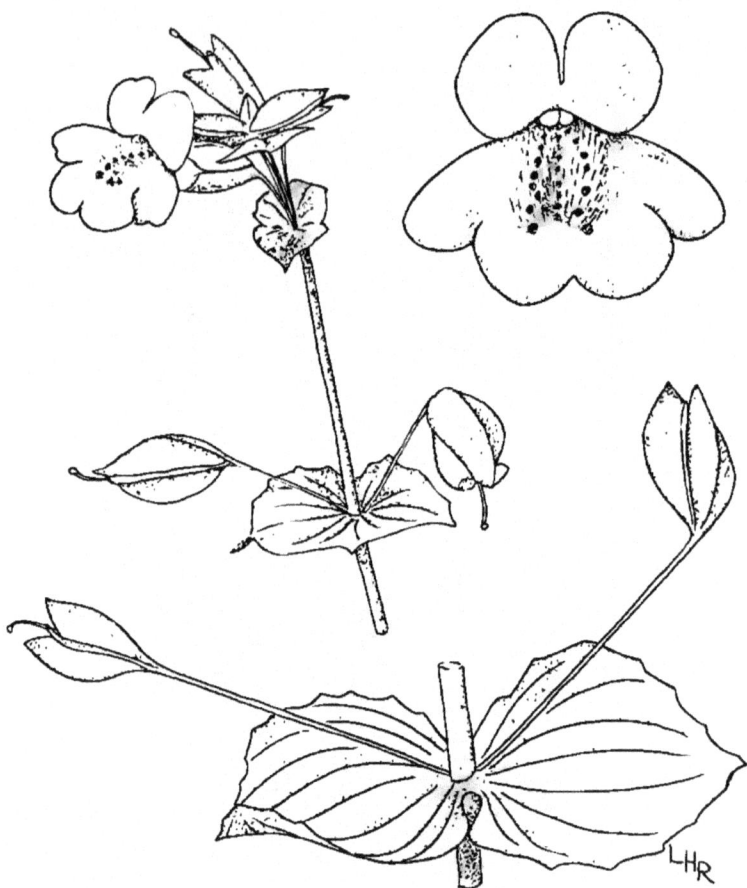

YELLOW MONKEY FLOWER

From Alaska to Arizona, yellow monkey flower blooms in the wet soil around springs, seeps, and streams. This 2–18 inch high perennial has bright yellow, snapdragonlike flowers with purple, brown, or red spots in the "throat." There are two lips; one above and one below the opening of the flower tube. The scientific name, *Mimulus,* was derived from the Latin word for mimic — referring to the grinning masks worn by ancient actors. The round to oval leaves are opposite and their edges are toothed. These leaves are edible; both Indians and settlers ate them raw as a salad green; in fact, the settlers called this plant "wild lettuce."

Mimulus guttatus   LOPSEED FAMILY

DESERT MARIGOLD

Even in the driest years, desert marigold's clear yellow flowers line the roadsides of the eastern Mohave Desert. The 1–2 inch wide flower heads appear from April to June, and again in early autumn. They have 20–30 ray flowers (see Picture Glossary) arranged in layers, with each ray having 3 rounded lobes at the end. Although noted for the flowers, this plant also has attractive silvery-green leaves covered with soft, wooly hair. They are mostly basal and are pinnately lobed. This species grows on well-drained, gravelly slopes and sandy plains to 5000 feet. Desert marigold makes a colorful addition to rock gardens.

Baileya multiradiata   ASTER FAMILY

DESERT GOLDEN POPPY

The fame of its cousin, California poppy (California's state flower), has eluded desert golden poppy. Why? Probably because it's tucked away in seldom-visited creosote-bush communities where few see it. Desert golden poppy is a brilliant yellow annual with 4 petals, each up to 1 inch long. Blooming from early spring until May, each plant sends up a few — to many — flower stalks. The 3-parted, deeply lobed leaves are clustered near the plant's base; the flowers are on leafless stalks. The fruit is a ribbed, slender capsule with many seeds. Desert golden poppy can be found in the low desert portions of canyons cutting into the Virgin Mountains, such as Sullivan's Canyon.

Eschscholzia glyptosperma   POPPY FAMILY

GOLDENEYE

Goldeneye's flowers look like miniature sunflowers. Blooming from June to September, this perennial's 1-1/2 inch flower head has bright yellow/golden ray and disk flowers borne on a well-rounded receptacle (see glossary). The leaves are broadly to narrowly lance-shaped, and are opposite except near the top of the plant, where they are alternate. This slender, 1 to 1-1/2 inch high herb can be found on open, rocky slopes at high elevations. In the Virgin Mountains, look for them atop Black Rock Mountain and along the Virgin Ridge. Sometimes classified as *Heliomeris multiflora*.

Viguiera multiflora ASTER FAMILY

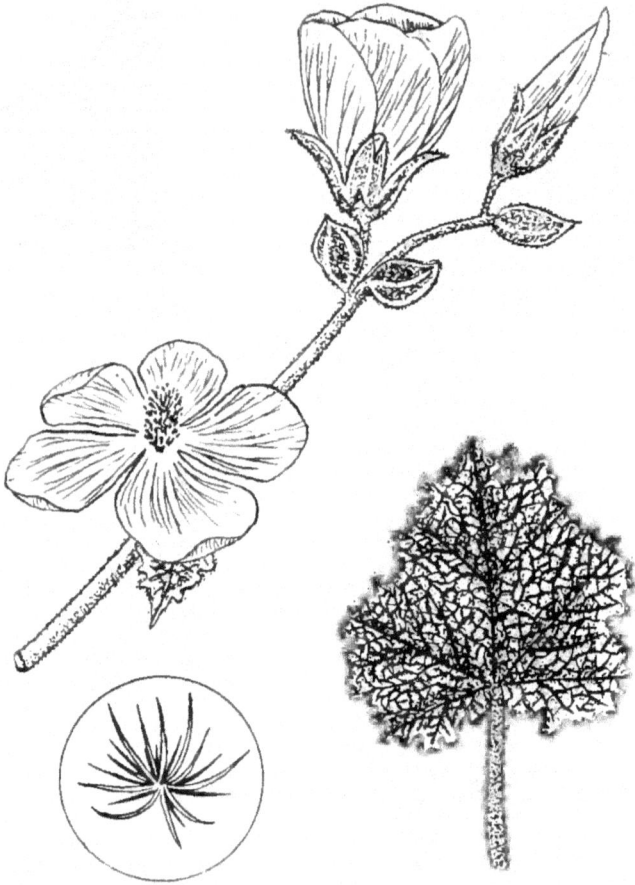

DESERT GLOBEMALLOW

Globemallow might be called "a sight for sore eyes." That's because its leaves and stem are covered with minute, star-shaped bristles that can severely irritate a person's eyes. This species is common in the Mohave Desert on dry, rocky slopes and along sandy washes. It is a woody-based perennial averaging 2 feet tall. The "peach red" blossoms have 5 petals, each 1/2 to 1 inch long. The thick deeply textured leaves are yellowish green and shallowly lobed. The Shoshones used the root of a related globemallow as a poultice, while the Hopis chewed the mucilaginous stems as a sort of "chewing gum."

Sphaeralcea ambigua   MALLOW FAMILY

SKYROCKET

Skyrocket's bright scarlet, 1 inch long, tubular flowers are built to attract their "favorite" pollinators: hummingbirds. (You, too, can attract hummingbirds by wearing red clothing.) This 1–3 foot tall biennial, with its clusters of red flowers, looks similar to firecracker penstemon, but unlike penstemon, the petals are flared outward about 1/4 inch and the leaves are deeply dissected into needle-like lobes. You'll find this species growing at pinyon-juniper and ponderosa pine elevations. It blooms from May to October. Skyrocket contains a detergent-like, poisonous chemical named saponin that was used by the Shoshone as a laxative. The Paiutes used the roots to produce a blue dye. Now sometimes classified as *Ipomopsis aggregata*.

Gilia aggregata   PHLOX FAMILY

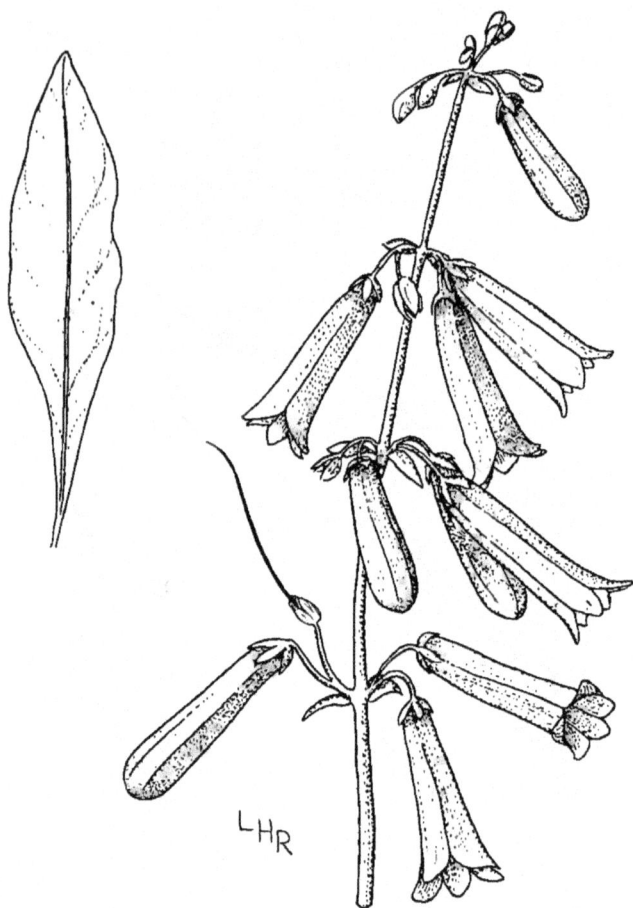

FIRECRACKER PENSTEMON

Roughly similar in appearance to skyrocket, firecracker penstemon has orange-red to scarlet, tubular flowers in terminal clusters that attract hummingbirds. There, the similarity ends, as firecracker penstemon's flowers do not end with flared petals (or they flare only slightly). Their shape invites a comparison to firecrackers. The yellowish stamens protrude slightly from the flower tubes. The leaves are opposite, thick, dark green, and not lobed. This perennial species grows 1–3 feet tall on gravelly desert slopes and among rocks to 7000 feet.

Penstemon eatonii   PLANTAIN FAMILY

DESERT PHLOX

Desert phlox grows in pincushion-like mounds on dry, open slopes and roadsides to 8000 feet. These 2–5 inch high mats are composed of many stems, and are covered with numerous white to pink or lavender flowers. Blooming March to May, these flowers have a slender, tubular throat flaring at the mouth into 5 "petals." The linear, sharp-pointed leaves are thickish, gray-green in color, and opposite. This plant is similar to the phloxes commonly planted in dry gardens; and is every bit as attractive.

Phlox austromontana   PHLOX FAMILY

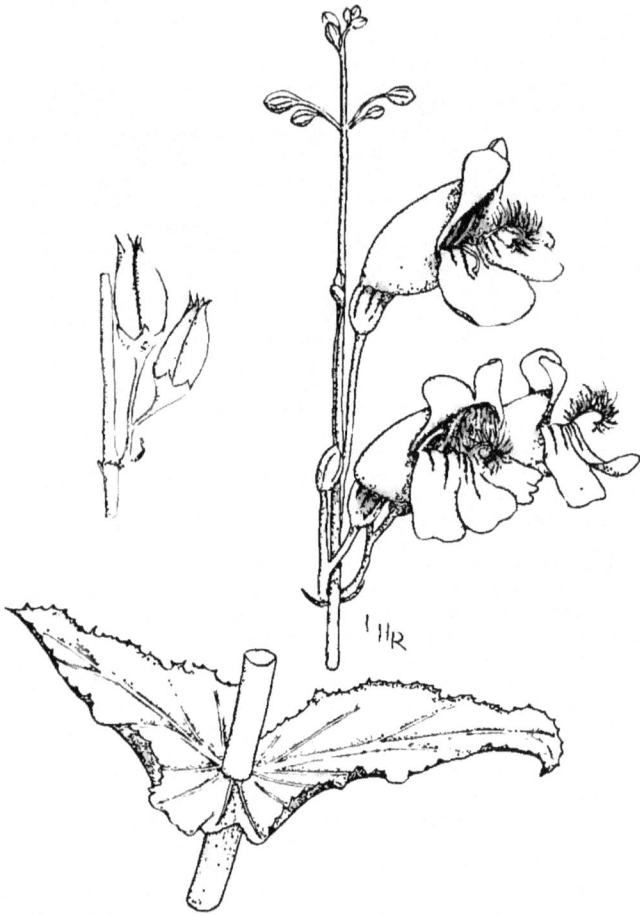

BEARD TONGUE

The strange name, beard tongue, refers to one of the stamens. Beard tongue has 5 stamens. Of these, one is sterile, thickened like a tongue, and covered with hairs. The fattened, white to pink (to "flesh" colored), fragrant flowers of beard tongue are conspicuous in the gravelly washes and roadsides of limestone rock areas from 3500 to 6000 feet. Blooming in May and June, this herbaceous perennial's flowers are 2-lipped, about 1 inch long, and nearly 1 inch wide. Prominent purple lines function to guide bees to the nectar and pollen. The leaves are grayish-green, opposite, and joined together around the 2–4 foot high stem.

Penstemon palmeri   PLANTAIN FAMILY

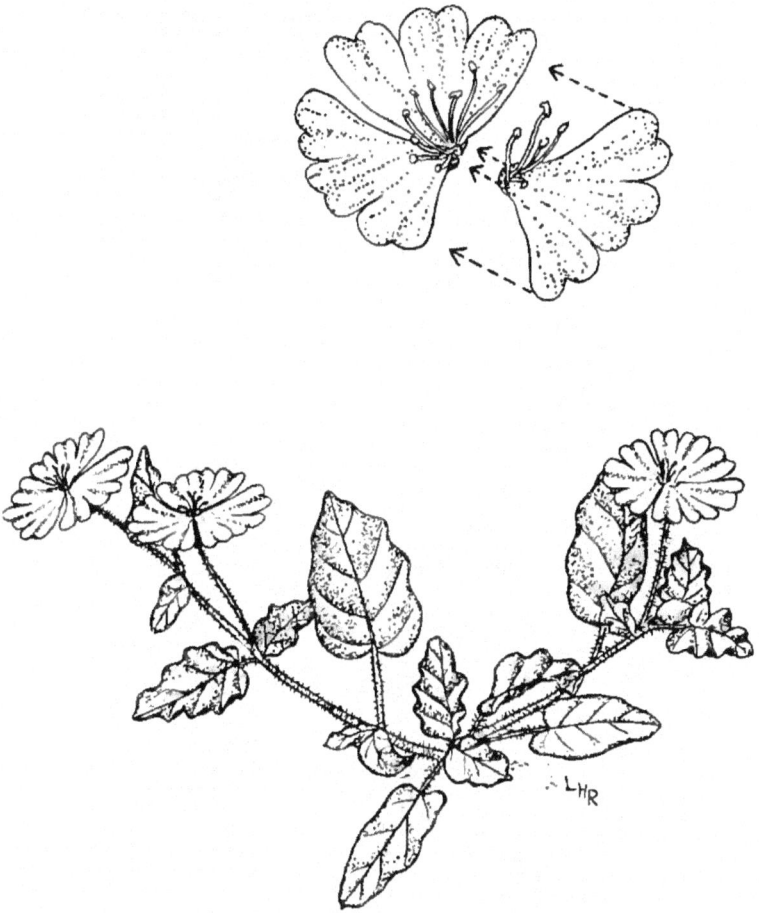

WINDMILLS

Whoever named this plant "windmills" took a good deal of poetic license, for the plant rarely feels the winds (the flower, however, does look somewhat like a windmill). It is a ground-hugging species with trailing, sticky, 6–30 inch long stems. The showy, rose-purple flowers can fool you. What looks to be a single 1/2 to 3/4 inch diameter flower is actually a cluster of 3 flowers. The flowers 1 can be seen from April to October. The leaves are opposite, with wavy edges and short petioles. Windmills is found in rocky or stony places to 5000 feet.

Allionia incarnata   FOUR-O'CLOCK FAMILY

WEAKSTEM MARIPOSA LILY

The Mariposa lilies are locally known as "Indian Onions" and "Indian Potatoes" because their bulbs were eaten by the Indians. The bulbs are said to be good either raw or steamed, but the flowers are so beautiful, most people would rather eat potatoes and save the lilies. Weakstem mariposa lily is named for its stem; which is so flexible, the flowers tend to lean on surrounding plants. The delicate, pinkish-white flowers have 3 petals; each with a yellow base. This plant is found from the low desert up through the pinyon-juniper zone in dry, brushy areas.

Calochortus flexuosus   LILY FAMILY

PURPLE SCORPIONWEED

Purple scorpionweed isn't nearly as fierce as its name. The foliage can cause dermatitis in some sensitive people, but the name comes from the shape of the flower-bearing structure rather than the "venom." Its spiral resembles the spiral of the scorpion's tail. Along this spiral, the purple flowers bloom in sequence. Each 1/2–3/4 inch wide flower has joined petals that converge into a narrow tube. The stamens protrude about 1/4 inch from the mouth of the tube. The alternate leaves have deep, rounded lobes. Purple scorpionweed can be found in the rocky wash bottom at the mouth of Mountain Sheep Wash.

Phacelia crenulata   BORAGE FAMILY

LARKSPUR

Sweet poison. The beautiful blue larkspur has been implicated in the widespread killing of range cattle. It contains several toxic alkaloids, including delphinine, which attack the nervous system. At one time, crews were employed in pulling up larkspurs. This perennial species grows to 2 feet tall in the openings between ponderosa pine trees on Black Rock Mountain. The bright blue, or sometimes blue and white, flowers are similar in shape to the common garden delphinium with their bilateral symmetry and spur extending 1 inch back from the flower's "face." The leaves are palmately divided, alternate, and clustered near the base of the stem. A related species grows at desert elevations.

Delphinium nuttallianum   BUTTERCUP FAMILY

CANAIGRE

Some plants are noted for beautiful flowers, others for beautiful fruits. Canaigre is among the latter. Its small, greenish flowers, borne on a 1–3 foot tall central stalk, are inconspicuous; but the rose-red fruits later found along the same stalk are quite beautiful. Canaigre is a perennial whose leaves first appear in February during mild winters. The 8–24 inch long, succulent leaves have wavy margins and their green color is often tinged with red. Canaigre is found in the deep, sandy soils of desert washes and plains below 6000 feet. Desert Indians ate the acidic leaves either roasted or boiled. The roots contain a high concentration of tannin and have been used by Indians for tanning leather.

Rumex hymenosepalus   BUCKWHEAT FAMILY

References

Andersen, Berniece A. "Use Of Native Plants In Early Mormon Country." In *Forms Upon The Frontier,* Ed. by Austin Fife, Alta Fife, and Henry H. Glassie. Logan, Utah: Utah State University Press Monograph Series (Volume XVI, Number 2), 1969.

Dodge, Natt N. 100 *Roadside Wildflowers of Southwest Uplands.* Globe, Arizona: Southwest Parks and Monuments Association, 1967.

Harlow, William M. and Ellwood S. Harrar. *Textbook of Dendrology.* New York: McGraw-Hill Book Company, 1968.

Jaeger, Edmund C. Desert Wild Flowers. Stanford, California: Stanford University Press, 1967.

Kearney, Thomas H., Robert H. Peebles, and collaborators. *Arizona Flora.* Berkeley, California: University of California Press, 1951.

Kingsbury, John M. *Deadly Harvest: A Guide to Common Poisonous Plants.* New York: Holt, Rinehart and Winston, 1965.

Kirk, Donald R. *Wild Edible Plants of the Western United States.* Healdsburg, California: Naturegraph Publishers, 1970.

Martin, Alexander C., Herbert S. Zim, and Arnold L. Nelson. *American Wildlife and Plants: A Guide to Wildlife Food Habits.* New York: Dover Publications, Inc., 1951.

Medsger, Oliver Perry. *Edible Wild Plants.* New York: The Macmillan Company, 1966.

Munz, Philip A. *California Desert Wildflowers.* Berkeley, California: University of California Press, 1962.

Murphey, Edith Van Allen. *Indian Uses of Native Plants.* Fort Bragg, California: Mendocino County Historical Society, 1959.

Nelson, Ruth Ashton. *Plants of Zion National Park.* Springdale, Utah: Zion Natural History Association, 1976.

Niethammer, Carolyn. *American Indian Food and Lore.* New York: Collier Books, 1974.

Parker, Kittie F. *An Illustrated Guide to Arizona Weeds.* Tucson, Arizona: The University of Arizona Press, 1972.

U. S. Department of Agriculture, Forest Service. *Range Plant Handbook.* Washington, D.C., 1937.

Index

Abies concolor, 19
Abronia fragans, 60
Agave utahensis, 46
Allionia incarnata, 77
Apacheplume, 27
Arctostaphylos patula, 35
Arctostaphylos pringlei, 35
Arctostaphylos pungens, 35
Arctostaphylos, 35
Argemone munita, 58
Arizona ash, 23
Arrow weed, 36
Baileya multiradiata, 69
Barrel cactus, 48
Beard tongue, 76
Beavertail cactus, 52
Blue yucca, 44
Buckhorn cholla, 49
Calochortus flexuosus, 78
Calochortus nuttallii, 56
Canaigre, 81
Cercis occidentalis, 41
Chilopsis linearis, 40
Cliff fendlerbush, 26
Cliffrose, 30
Coleogyne ramosissima, 31
Cowania mexicana, 30
Creosote bush, 32
Dalea fremontii, 42
Datura wrightii, 61
Delphinium nuttallianum, 80
Desert globemallow, 72
Desert golden poppy, 70

Desert marigold, 69
Desert phlox, 75
Desert trumpet, 66
Desert willow, 40
Dixie blackbrush, 31
Douglas fir, 18
Echinocereus engelmannii, 55
Echinocereus mojavensis, 51
Echinocereus triglochidiatus, 51
Ephedra, 21
Eriogonum inflatum, 66
Eschscholzia glyptosperma, 70
Eucnide urens, 29
Evening primrose, 59
Fallugia paradoxa, 27
Fendlera rupicola, 26
Ferocactus cylindraceus, 48
Firecracker penstemon, 74
Fishhook cactus, 54
Foothill deathcamas, 63
Fragrant sand verbena, 60
Fraxinus velutina, 23
Fremont cottonwood, 22
Gambel oak, 25
Gilia aggregata, 73
Golden cholla, 47
Goldeneye, 71
Grizzly bear cactus, 53
Ground cherry, 64
Hedgehog cactus, 51
Honey mesquite, 34
Indigo bush, 42
Joshua tree, 43

Juniperus osteosperma, 20
Larkspur, 80
Larrea tridentata, 32
Lithophragma tenellum, 57
Mammillaria tetrancistra, 54
Manzanita, 35
Mimulus guttatus, 68
Mormon tea, 21
Mortonia utahensis, 28
Mortonia, 28
Nasturtium officinale, 62
New Mexican locust, 38
Oenothera caespitosa, 59
Oenothera multijuga, 65
Opuntia acanthocarpa, 49
Opuntia basilaris, 52
Opuntia echinocarpa, 47
Opuntia phaeacantha, 50
Opuntia polyacantha, 53
Opuntia, 50
Penstemon eatonii, 74
Penstemon palmeri, 76
Phacelia crenulata, 79
Phlox austromontana, 75
Physalis crassifolia, 64
Pinus monophylla, 17
Pinus ponderosa, 16
Pinyon pine, 17
Pluchea sericea, 36
Ponderosa pine, 16
Populus deltoides, 22
Prickly poppy, 58
Princesplume, 67
Prosopis juliflora, 34
Pseudotsuga menziesii, 18
Purple scorpionweed, 79
Purple torch cactus, 55

Purshia mexicana, 30
Quercus gambelii, 25
Quercus turbinella, 24
Rhus trilobata, 33
Robinia neomexicana, 38
Rock nettle, 29
Rosa, 39
Rumex hymenosepalus, 81
Running opuntia, 50
Sacred datura, 61
Sego lily, 56
Shrub live oak, 24
Silver cholla, 47
Skyrocket, 73
Slender woodland star, 57
Sphaeralcea ambigua, 72
Squawbush, 33
Stanleya pinnata, 67
Tamarisk, 37
Tamarix chinensis, 37
Utah agave, 46
Utah juniper, 20
Utah yucca, 45
Viguiera multiflora, 71
Watercress, 62
Weakstem mariposa lily, 78
Western redbud, 41
White fir, 19
Wild rose, 39
Windmills, 77
Yellow day primrose, 65
Yellow monkey flower, 68
Yucca baccata, 44
Yucca brevifolia, 43
Yucca elata, 45
Zigadenus paniculatus, 63

Removing Plants

Spiny desert plants can protect themselves from natural enemies, but not from people with shovels. To protect these plants, some of which are threatened by over-collecting, Arizona has a law requiring collectors to obtain a permit before digging up these plants:

> Joshua tree
> *all* cactus species
> western redbud
> *all* yucca species
> Utah agave (century plant)

This law is rigidly enforced by Arizona police. Violators can be fined and/or imprisoned. More information on Arizona's many protected plants is available at:

> https://agriculture.az.gov/protected-arizona-native-plants

Since the Virgin Mountains are administered by the Bureau of Land Management, permission must be obtained from them before removing any plant. The local office is:

> United States Department of the Interior
> Bureau of Land Management
> Arizona Strip District Office
> 345 East Riverside Drive
> St. George, Utah 84790
> www.blm.gov/az/st/en/fo/arizona_strip_field.html

U.S. Department of the Interior
Bureau of Land Management
Arizona Strip District

The Bureau of Land Management administers about 473 million acres of public land in the western states and Alaska. As an agency of the Department of the Interior, BLM is charged with managing these lands in the public interest to ensure a continuing supply of recreation, minerals, range, wildlife, water and timber. As part of this comprehensive resource management program, environmental education efforts have been initiated to acquaint people with their natural environments.